# SCRIPTURES FOR WORSHIP, HOLINESS, AND THE NATURE OF GOD

THE TOPICAL SCRIPTURE SERIES

SCRIPTURES FOR

# WORSHIP, HOLINESS,

AND

# THE NATURE OF GOD

## JOHN ECKHARDT

CHARISMA
HOUSE

Most CHARISMA HOUSE BOOK GROUP products are available at special quantity discounts for bulk purchase for sales promotions, premiums, fund-raising, and educational needs. For details, write Charisma House Book Group, 600 Rinehart Road, Lake Mary, Florida 32746, or telephone (407) 333-0600.

SCRIPTURES FOR WORSHIP, HOLINESS, AND THE NATURE OF GOD
  by John Eckhardt
Published by Charisma House
Charisma Media/Charisma House Book Group
600 Rinehart Road
Lake Mary, Florida 32746
www.charismahouse.com

Visit the author's website at www.johneckhardt.global.

Library of Congress Cataloging-in-Publication Data:
An application to register this book for cataloging has been
submitted to the Library of Congress.
International Standard Book Number: 978-1-62999-493-2
E-book ISBN: 978-1-62999-494-9

Parts of this book were previously published by Charisma House as
*Prophetic Activation*, ISBN: 978-1-62998-709-5 and *Ordinary People,
Extraordinary Power*, ISBN: 978-1-61638-166-0.

This publication is translated in Spanish under the title *Escrituras
para la adoración, la santidad y la naturaleza de Dios*, copyright ©
2018 by John Eckhardt, published by Casa Creación, a Charisma
Media company. All rights reserved.

18 19 20 21 22 — 987654321
Printed in the United States of America

# CONTENTS

## Introduction

# WORSHIPPING IN THE BEAUTY OF HIS HOLINESS

*Worship the LORD in the beauty of holiness;*
*tremble before Him, all the earth.*

—PSALM 96:9

Psalm 96 is a beautiful prophetic psalm that foretells the establishment of the new covenant and the coming of the kingdom of God. It is also a psalm that raises the importance of worship, holiness, and the manifestation of the glory of God's character. As we prepare to explore these concepts, I want to provide some revelatory foundation and teaching that we will build on throughout the book.

Perhaps like me, you've read this psalm so many times before but didn't immediately understand some things. After studying it for some time and praying for understanding, the Lord revealed to me some important aspects about who He is and what He did through Jesus that I believe His people need to know. Let's take a look.

Psalm 96:6–10 says,

> Honor and majesty are before Him;
>> strength and beauty are in His sanctuary.
> Give unto the LORD, O families of the people,
>> give unto the LORD glory and strength.
> Give unto the LORD the glory due His name;
>> bring an offering, and come into His courts.
> Worship the LORD in the beauty of holiness;
>> tremble before Him, all the earth.
> Say among the nations, "The LORD reigns!
> Indeed, the world is established; it shall not be
>> moved;
>> He shall judge the peoples righteously."

Verse 10 is where I would always stop. I could not figure out what it meant. What does it mean that the world is established? Isn't the world already established? Are we living now in an unestablished world? Or is the verse referring to something to come? If so, how shall it be established? I understood the part of the verse that talks about the reign of God. It means the rule of God, the kingdom of God. It's prophetic—a word concerning when God would come to rule and reign on the earth. Let me explain.

The Bible is a covenantal book. Each testament—old and new—represents the old covenant and new covenant. I believe this verse is a prophetic picture of when the new covenant world would be established with the coming of Christ. When He came, He said, "The time is fulfilled, and the kingdom of God is at hand. Repent and believe the gospel" (Mark 1:15). And God established this new covenant world that we live in now, which is a world of salvation, righteousness, the move of the Holy Spirit, and worship. This is the world you now experience. This verse is not talking about some physical world being established. It is talking about the world we live in covenantally.

Where you are now—experiencing praise, worship, the Holy Spirit, prophecy, miracles, healings, the presence of God, righteousness, salvation, and joy—is the world that God established through His covenant.

## Beholding the Beauty of God

Some time ago I was conducting a home-going service. One of the speakers said the person who had died had gone to a better place and left us in this ugly world. I had to stop and think about that. Many people think of the world as an ugly place. I agree that there is some ugliness here, but there is also some beauty here. We forget that we are not just here waiting for God to come and change everything, but we can take hold of all the blessings of the kingdom now. Jesus came that we may have life and have it more abundantly—and that is not something we wait for till the sweet by and by. We can worship God and experience the beauty of holiness on this earth now.

Think about this. Where is the beauty of God according to Psalm 96:6? It is in His sanctuary, in His temple. Because of the indwelling Holy Spirit, we are the sanctuary of God. We're the temple of God.

> Do you not know that your body is the temple of the Holy Spirit, who is in you, whom you have received from God?
>
> —1 CORINTHIANS 6:19

It is also that when you come to the physical house of God and you begin to worship, you encounter the beauty of God. When you encounter the beauty of God, it makes life worth living. So many people feel that life is so hard for them and so ugly. It is because they've not experienced the beauty of God in the sanctuary. But for us, when we come to worship and we come into contact with God's beauty, God's glory, God's majesty, and God's character, it is a spiritual thing. You cannot see it with the natural eye, but there is a spiritual realm of beauty that you encounter as a covenant believer.

God is beautiful. Heaven is beautiful. God is full of glory and majesty. God is the most beautiful person in the universe. He's the one who created everything on the earth that is beautiful. You need to have a revelation of this spiritual realm of beauty in your life, because beauty does something to your spirit. People will spend a million dollars for one piece of art just because it's beautiful. They'll spend all kinds of money to decorate their homes with beautiful things—beautiful carpet, furniture, and other items. We'll get on an airplane and fly hundreds of miles to beautiful places, to see a beautiful beach or mountains. We'll buy a nice, beautiful car or beautiful clothing. We like nice, beautiful things, because beauty does something to our spirits.

No one wants to live in an ugly house, wear ugly clothes, or go to ugly places. Ugly is depressing. When I say ugly, I'm not only referring to outward ugliness. There are people who have ugly spirits and attitudes who can't experience beauty from within or in the world around them. You can be beautiful on the outside and ugly on the inside.

## Encountering the Presence of God

The new covenant world that God established is a world where you can encounter God's beauty and strength in the sanctuary, in worship. This is the world that He came to establish. You are now living in that new covenant world. I don't know about you, but when I think of the world that God established for me—a new covenant world of salvation, healing, deliverance, beauty, worship, glory, praise, and sacrifice to God—I can't help but to see His beauty all around me. I live in the new covenant world. I'm in this physical world, but I also inhabit another world—a spiritual world that God rules and reigns no matter what is happening on this planet. His lovingkindness and tender mercies are new every morning. When you look around and see things such as war, terror attacks, mass killings, devastating natural disasters, and premature death, it can be hard to see the beauty of God. Some of us may start to wonder where God is and how we can live in a world of murder, devastation, and pain.

We have to be careful in these cases that we don't see only the natural and physical realm and neglect the spiritual, new covenant world—the world of salvation, joy, peace, and righteousness. Sometimes I don't think we recognize what we have in God. We take the power and presence of God for granted. Encountering God in worship, bowing and lifting our hands, being partakers in the glory of God, hearing the voice of God, and coming in contact with God's majesty and beauty—what a life to live! I've become so used to this life, I could not live without it. It's what makes me breathe and live and enjoy life.

## Enjoying God

I enjoy being saved, because I enjoy God. I enjoy His character, His holiness, and His ways. A life with God is to be enjoyed, and He wants to enjoy us. He established a spiritual world for us that we can step into through salvation, where we can touch God's glory, His anointing, His joy, His peace, His shalom, His favor, His blessing, His prosperity, His wealth, His anointing, His presence,

His power, His glory, and so much more. If people only knew!

People have been bombarded with so much religion they think that's what serving God is about. But God didn't come to set up a religion; He came to create a new world, a new order, and a new place in the spirit, not religion. If people only knew the joy, peace, prosperity, and rest they can have, they would have life and that more abundantly. If they only knew the greatness of God when He reveals Himself to them, how they can enjoy God and being in the kingdom of God, and how they can enjoy being with His people in a worshipping church. They could experience such freedom if they only knew!

God reigns and the world is established. We live in a new covenant world of salvation and righteousness through Christ, and it cannot be moved. I don't care how many devils and demons attack. They will never be able to move this new covenant world. It's from generation to generation to generation. It will never end. It is an unmovable kingdom that cannot be shaken. No matter if the earth quakes, and tsunamis, hurricanes, and tornados come, this world is established. Your salvation and mine are established. It is set. That's why we praise God the way we do. We have something that is unshakable. We don't have to worry about the kingdom being overthrown and shaken. Nations may rise, and nations may fall. Governments and people may come and go. But there's one thing that continues from generation to generation, and it is the Spirit of God and the new covenant. Forgiveness, redemption, and the blood of Jesus will never lose their power.

God is the same yesterday, today, and forever. When I go to bed at night, I never have to wonder if God will still be on the throne when I wake up. When I go to bed, He's on the throne. And when I wake up, He's on the throne. In the morning, at noon, and at night, He's on the throne. He's always there. If I call upon Him, He will answer me. Psalm 121:4 says He who keeps Israel will never slumber nor sleep. God never goes to sleep. There's never a "Do not disturb" sign on heaven's door. God is always there. He is faithful and good and kind. That's enough to praise God for, and that's what the study of the scriptures presented in this book are all about—worshipping God in all of His beauty, majesty, and splendor.

## Meditating on God

Many years ago, the Lord led me to find key scriptures on healing, deliverance, and warfare and turn them in to short prayers. He told me that these prayers have power against the enemy when prayed, because they are based in the supernatural power of the Word of God. As I developed these prayers and declarations and used them in ministry, we began to see that praying the Word had tremendous power to heal and deliver people from all kinds of bondages. My book *Prayers That Rout Demons* and the others in that series developed out of this season of ministry. To this day we get reports of people being healed and delivered because of these short prayers.

But now the Lord has led me to do something new. He has instructed me to develop topical resource on various principles of God and His kingdom to help people focus in on what they need from God's Word specifically. What you have in your hand is a combination of scriptures on worship, holiness, and the nature of God from both the Old Testament and the New Testament. I encourage you to take these verses and add them to your times of prayer, worship, and meditation. They will help you develop the discipline to use the power of God's Word to build faith for breakthrough, to get to know God more intimately, and to walk uprightly before Him.

In each section I will break down how worship, holiness, and the character of God are expressed in each of the testaments, including some examples of the manifestations of the opposite traits. I will also break down the Hebrew and Greek meanings of the key words related to each topic to build greater understanding and stronger faith.

I pray that as you read this book, God will bring you to a place of confidence in His desire to save you and give you an abundant life. It is my firm belief that believers do not have to wait until the sweet by and by to experience the beauty and wonders of God. I believe He has established a world for us to experience and enjoy Him in right here and now.

By gaining a fuller understanding of God's character and His heart toward people, our levels of worship will rise throughout the earth realm, and an increase of the manifestation of God's glory will be shown throughout this age and the age to come. Let's go now and inquire of the Lord.

> One thing I have asked from the LORD, that will I seek after—for me to dwell in the house of the LORD all the days of my life, to see the beauty of the LORD, and to inquire in His temple.
>
> —PSALM 27:4

# PART I

# **WORSHIP**
## SCRIPTURES

# 1

# IN SPIRIT AND IN TRUTH

The institution of worship in the Bible began with King David's establishment of Israel's 24/7 worship. He set up a tabernacle—a tent erected to house the ark of the covenant—to be the place for uninterrupted praise and worship to God (1 Chron. 15–17). Courses of priests were set in the tabernacle to praise the Lord and offer new songs to Him continually. The worship was led by three prophetic families—the families of Asaph, Heman, and Jeduthun (1 Chron. 25:1–7). Each family consisted of prophets and seers who played instruments and sang prophetically. Many of the psalms were birthed and written during this time. These psalms were prophetic and declared the will and purposes of God.

The tabernacle of David is a type of the New Testament church. What he established in physical Jerusalem was a shadow of what we have now in the kingdom. The New Testament church, now indwelled and empowered by the

Holy Spirit, should also be a prophetic family of prophets and those who prophesy by the Holy Spirit (Acts 2:18).

In establishing the order of worship for the nation of Israel, David, an Old Testament man, was able to taste the power of the age to come (Heb. 6:5). David was able to receive a revelation from heaven and establish it upon the earth.

## A New Age of Worship

The prophetic anointing increases the level of worship. A study of the evolution of worship—from the Old Testament to the New—shows that we have moved to the age of the kingdom, where worship is done by spirit and truth. The kingdom is spiritual, the church is a spiritual house, and the church consists of spiritual people who offer spiritual sacrifices. We have come to Zion, the mountain of God. We have come to Zion, the habitation of God. We drink of the river that flows from Zion. We are a people who draw strength from the presence of God. We love the presence of God. We love dwelling in Zion. We minister from the strength of Zion. We rule and reign with Christ in Zion.

This is new covenant worship. This is prophetic worship. This is the new wineskin that holds the new wine.

In this first section I have pulled together all the scriptures from the Old Testament to the New Testament that focus on the transition from old covenant worship to new covenant worship—from physical sacrifices to spiritual.

The scriptures show both godly and ungodly manifestations of worship, giving you both examples to emulate and ones to avoid. I will also break down the Hebrew and Greek meanings of the key words related to each topic to build greater understanding and stronger faith.

The following verses are key for this section:

> O sing unto the LORD a new song: sing unto the LORD, all the earth!
>
> —PSALM 96:1

> The hour is coming, and is now here, when the true worshippers will worship the Father in spirit and truth. For the Father seeks such to worship Him. God is Spirit, and those who worship Him must worship Him in spirit and truth.
>
> —JOHN 4:23–24

# 2

# WORSHIP IN THE OLD TESTAMENT

Worship in the Old Testament is characterized by the building of the sanctuary to house the ark of the covenant, the Levitical priesthood, King David's 24/7 worship, and finally King Solomon's temple. The Old Testament is where God established through David the preeminence of worship for His people.

The Hebrew words used in the Old Testament to express various streams and styles of worship and praise are:[1]

- *Shachah* (Ps. 29:2)—to depress or prostrate in homage or loyalty to God, bow down, fall down flat

- *Barak* (Ps. 34:1)—to kneel or bow, to give reverence to God as an act of adoration, implies a continual conscious giving place to God, to be attuned to Him and His presence

6

- *Halal* (Ps. 22:23)—to praise, to make a show or rave about, to glory in or boast upon, to be clamorously foolish about your adoration of God (as in *hallelujah*)

- *Tehillah* (Ps. 34:1)—to sing *hallal*, a new song, a hymn of spontaneous praise glorifying God in song

- *Todah* (Ps. 50:14)—an extension of the hand, avowal, adoration, a choir of worshippers, confession, sacrifice of praise, thanksgiving

- *Yadah* (Ps. 33:2)—to use, hold out the hand, to throw (a stone or arrow) at or away, to revere or worship (with extended hands, praise, thankful, thanksgiving)

- *Zamar* (Ps. 66:2)—to touch the strings or parts of a musical instrument, i.e., to play upon it, to make music accompanied by the voice, to celebrate in song and music, give praise, sing forth praises, psalms

## Genesis

Abraham said to his young men, "Stay here with the donkey. The boy and I will go over there and worship and then return to you."

—Genesis 22:5

Then the man bowed down his head and worshipped the LORD.

—GENESIS 24:26

And I bowed down my head and worshipped the LORD, and blessed the LORD God of my master Abraham, who had led me in the right way to take the daughter of my master's brother for his son.

—GENESIS 24:48

When Abraham's servant heard their words, he worshipped the LORD, bowing himself to the earth.

—GENESIS 24:52

She conceived again and gave birth to a son, and she said, "Now I will praise the LORD!" Therefore she called his name Judah. Then she stopped giving birth.

—GENESIS 29:35

## Exodus

And the people believed. And when they heard that the LORD had visited the children of Israel and that He had looked on their affliction, they bowed down and worshipped.

—EXODUS 4:31

That you shall say, "It is the sacrifice of the LORD's Passover, who passed over the houses of the children of Israel in Egypt, when He smote the Egyptians, and delivered our households." And the people bowed down and worshipped.

—EXODUS 12:27

Then He said to Moses, "Come up to the LORD, you, and Aaron, Nadab, and Abihu, and seventy of the elders of Israel, and you shall worship from a distance."

—EXODUS 24:1

They have quickly turned aside from the way which I commanded them. They have made for themselves a molded calf, and have worshipped it, and have sacrificed to it, and said, "This is your god, O Israel, which has brought you up from the land of Egypt."

—EXODUS 32:8

When all the people saw the pillar of cloud standing at the entrance of the tent, all the people rose up and worshipped, every man at the entrance of his tent.

—EXODUS 33:10

Moses made haste and bowed to the ground and worshipped.

—EXODUS 34:8

For you shall not worship any other god, for the LORD, whose name is Jealous, is a jealous God.

—EXODUS 34:14

## Numbers

But truly as I live, all the earth will be filled with the glory of the Lord.

—Numbers 14:21

## Deuteronomy

And beware, lest you lift up your eyes to heaven, and when you see the sun, and the moon, and the stars, even all the host of heaven, you are led astray and worship them, and serve them, that which the Lord your God has allotted to all nations under the whole heaven.

—Deuteronomy 4:19

If you ever forget the Lord your God and go after other gods and serve them and worship them, then I testify against you today that you will surely perish.

—Deuteronomy 8:19

Take heed to yourselves that your heart be not deceived, and you turn away and serve other gods and worship them.

—Deuteronomy 11:16

And has gone and served other gods and worshipped them, either the sun, or moon, or any of the host of heaven, which I have not commanded.

—Deuteronomy 17:3

"Now, indeed, I have brought the first fruits of the land, which you, O Lord, have given me." Then you must set it before the LORD your God and worship before the LORD your God.

—DEUTERONOMY 26:10

For they went and served other gods, and worshipped them, gods which they did not know and which He had not given to them.

—DEUTERONOMY 29:26

But if your heart turns away, so that you do not obey, but are drawn away, and worship other gods and serve them, then I declare to you today that you will surely perish and that you will not prolong your days.

—DEUTERONOMY 30:17–18

This is the blessing to Judah. He said: Listen, O LORD, to the voice of Judah, and bring him to his people; may his hands contend for them, and may You help him against his enemies.

—DEUTERONOMY 33:7

## Joshua

He said, "Neither, for I am the commander of the army of the Lord. Now I have come." Then Joshua fell with his face to the ground and worshipped. Then he said, "What does my Lord wish to say to His servant?"

—JOSHUA 5:14

## Judges

After the death of Joshua, the children of Israel inquired of the LORD, "Who should go up against the Canaanites first, in order to wage war against them?" The LORD said, "Judah shall go up. Indeed, I have given the land into their hands."

—JUDGES 1:1–2

When Gideon heard the telling of the dream and its interpretation, he worshipped, returned to the camp of Israel, and said, "Get up, for the LORD has given the Midianite camp into your hands."

—JUDGES 7:15

## 1 Samuel

This man went up out of his city annually to worship and to sacrifice to the LORD of Hosts in Shiloh. And there the two sons of Eli, Hophni and Phinehas, were priests to the LORD.

—1 SAMUEL 1:3

They rose up in the morning early and worshipped before the LORD. And they returned and came to their house to Ramah. And Elkanah knew Hannah his wife, and the LORD remembered her.

—1 SAMUEL 1:19

"Therefore also I have let the LORD have him. As long as he lives he will be dedicated to the LORD." And he worshipped the LORD there.

—1 SAMUEL 1:28

After that you will come to the hill of God, where the garrison of the Philistines is. And when you come there to the city, you will meet a group of prophets coming down from the high place with a harp, a tambourine, a flute, and a lyre before them. And they will prophesy.

—1 SAMUEL 10:5

Now therefore, please pardon my sin and return with me, that I may worship the Lord.

—1 SAMUEL 15:25

## 2 Samuel

So David did not allow the ark of the LORD to be brought to him in the City of David. Instead, David redirected it to the house of Obed-Edom the Gittite. The ark of the LORD remained at the house of Obed-Edom the Gittite for three months, and the LORD blessed Obed-Edom and his entire household.

—2 SAMUEL 6:10–11

So David arose from the ground, washed, anointed himself, and changed his garments. Then he entered the house of the LORD and worshipped. He then went in to his own house. When he asked, they set down food for him and ate.

—2 SAMUEL 12:20

When David came to the summit where he would worship God, Hushai the Arkite approached him with his coat torn and dirt on his head.

—2 SAMUEL 15:32

Now these be the last words of David. David the son of Jesse said, and the man who was raised up on high, the anointed of the God of Jacob, and the sweet psalmist of Israel, said, The Spirit of the LORD spake by me, and his word was in my tongue.

—2 SAMUEL 23:1–2, KJV

## 1 Kings

But if you and your sons turn in any way from following Me and do not keep My commandments and My statutes which I have set before you, but go and serve other gods and worship them, then I will cut Israel out of the land which I have given them, and I will cast this house, which I have consecrated for My name, out of My sight, and Israel shall be a proverb and a byword among all people.

—1 KINGS 9:6–7

And they will answer, "Because they forsook the LORD their God, who brought their fathers out of the land of Egypt, and took hold of other gods and have worshipped and served them. That is why the LORD has brought all this disaster upon them."

—1 KINGS 9:9

I will tear the kingdom out of the hand of Solomon...because they have forsaken Me and have worshipped Ashtoreth the goddess of the Sidonians, Chemosh the god of the Moabites, and Molech the god of the children of Ammon and have not walked in My ways and have not done that which is right in My eyes, to keep My statutes and judgments, as his father David had done.

—1 KINGS 11:31–33

This was a sin, for the people went to worship before the one, even all the way in Dan.

—1 KINGS 12:30

The sins of Jeroboam the son of Nebat were seen as minor for him to walk in, for he took Jezebel the daughter of Ethbaal, king of the Sidonians, as his wife and went and served Baal and worshipped him.

—1 KINGS 16:31

For he served Baal and worshipped him and provoked the LORD God of Israel to anger, according to all that his father had done.

—1 KINGS 22:53

## 2 Kings

"Now call to me all the prophets of Baal, all his worshippers, and all his priests. Let none go unaccounted for, because I have a great sacrifice for Baal. All who are not accounted for will not live." But Jehu did it with cunning in order to destroy the servants of Baal.

—2 Kings 10:19

Rather, the Lord, who brought you up out of the land of Egypt with great power and an outstretched arm, Him you shall fear, to Him you shall bow down, and to Him you shall sacrifice.

—2 Kings 17:36

He went back and rebuilt the high places that Hezekiah his father had destroyed. He erected altars for Baal, made an Asherah pole as Ahab king of Israel had done, and worshipped all the host of heaven and served them.

—2 Kings 21:3

He walked in all the ways that his father walked, served the idols that his father served, and worshipped them.

—2 Kings 21:21

## 1 Chronicles

David was dressed in a fine linen robe, as were all the Levites who carried the ark, the Levites who

were singers, and Chenaniah, the leader of the
musicians' prophetic songs. David also wore a
linen ephod.

—1 Chronicles 15:27, nog

So they brought in the ark of God, placed it in the
midst of the tent that David had erected for it, and
drew near to God with burnt offerings and peace
offerings. When David had finished offering the
burnt offerings and the peace offerings, he blessed
the people in the name of the Lord. Then he dis-
tributed to all the children of Israel, both men and
women, a loaf of bread, a piece of meat, and a raisin
cake for each.

And he appointed some of the Levites to minister
before the ark of the Lord, to commemorate, to
thank, and to praise the Lord God of Israel: Asaph
the chief, and next to him Zechariah, then Jeiel,
Shemiramoth, Jehiel, Mattithiah, Eliab, Benaiah,
and Obed-Edom: Jeiel with stringed instruments
and harps, but Asaph made music with the cymbals.
Moreover, Benaiah and Jahaziel the priests sounded
trumpets continually before the ark of the covenant
of God.

On that day then, David delivered for the first
time this psalm of thanksgiving to the Lord into
the hand of Asaph and his brothers:

Give thanks to the Lord, call on His name;
    make known His deeds among the peoples.
Sing to Him, sing praise to Him,

recount all His wonders.
Glory in His holy name;
    let the heart of those who seek the Lord rejoice.
Seek the Lord and His strength;
    seek His face continually.
Remember His wonders which He has done,
    His wonders and the judgments of His mouth.

—1 Chronicles 16:1–12

Sing to the Lord, all the earth.
    Proclaim good tidings of His salvation from day
        to day.
Declare His glory among the nations,
    His wonders among all the peoples.
For great is the Lord and greatly to be praised.
    He is to be feared above all gods.
For all the gods of the peoples are idols,
    but the Lord made the heavens.
Honor and majesty are before Him;
    strength and joy are in His place.
Give to the Lord, O families of the peoples,
    give to the Lord glory and strength.
Give to the Lord the glory due His name;
    bring an offering and come before Him,
    bow down to the Lord in holy array.
Tremble before Him, all the earth.
The world also is firmly established; it shall not
    be moved.
Let the heavens rejoice, and let the earth be glad.
Let them say among the nations, "The Lord
    is King."

Let the sea roar, and all its fullness.
Let the field rejoice, and all that is in it.
Then the trees of the forest will ring out before
    the LORD,
    for He is coming to judge the earth.
Oh, give thanks to the LORD, for He is good;
    for His mercy endures forever.
Now say, "Save us, O God of our salvation,
    and gather us and deliver us from the nations,
    that we may give thanks to Your holy name,
    to glory in Your praise.
Blessed is the LORD, the God of Israel,
    from everlasting to everlasting."
Then all the people said, "Amen," and "Praise
    the LORD."

So he left Asaph and his brothers before the ark of the covenant of the LORD to minister before the ark regularly, as each day required, and also Obed-Edom and his sixty-eight brothers, while Obed-Edom, the son of Jeduthun, and Hosah were to be gatekeepers.

And he left Zadok the priest and his priestly brothers before the tabernacle of the LORD at the high place that was at Gibeon to offer burnt offerings to the LORD on the altar of burnt offering continually, morning and evening, according to all that was written in the Law of the LORD, which He commanded Israel.

With them were Heman and Jeduthun and the rest who were chosen, who were marked by name to give thanks to the LORD, for His mercy endures forever. Heman and Jeduthun had with them trumpets and cymbals to sound aloud and instruments for sacred song. The sons of Jeduthun were appointed to the gate.

Then all the people departed, each man to his house, and David returned to bless his house.

—1 CHRONICLES 16:23–43

Honor and majesty are before Him; strength and joy are in His place.

—1 CHRONICLES 16:27

Give to the LORD the glory due His name; bring an offering and come before Him, bow down to the LORD in holy array.

—1 CHRONICLES 16:29

Then David and the officers of the army also set apart for the service some of the sons of Asaph, and of Heman, and of Jeduthun, those who prophesied with lyres, harps, and cymbals. The number of those who did the work according to their service was:

From the sons of Asaph:

Zakkur, Joseph, Nethaniah, and Asarelah, the sons of Asaph under the guidance of Asaph, who prophesied according to the decree of the king.

For Jeduthun, the sons of Jeduthun:

Gedaliah, Zeri, Jeshaiah, Hashabiah, and Mattithiah, six, under the guidance of their father Jeduthun, who prophesied with the lyre in giving thanks and praise to the LORD.

For Heman, the sons of Heman:

Bukkiah, Mattaniah, Uzziel, Shubael and Jerimoth, Hananiah, Hanani, Eliathah, Giddalti, and Romamti-Ezer, Joshbekashah, Mallothi, Hothir, Mahazioth. All these were the sons of Heman, the king's seer, according to the words of God, to exalt him, for God gave fourteen sons and three daughters to Heman.

—1 CHRONICLES 25:1–5

Therefore David blessed the LORD in the sight of all the assembly and said, "Blessed (praised, adored, and thanked) are You, O LORD God of Israel (Jacob) our father, forever and ever.

—1 CHRONICLES 29:10, AMP

Then David said to all the assembly, "Bless now the LORD your God." So all the assembly blessed the LORD, the God of their fathers. They bowed down and paid homage to the LORD and the king.

—1 CHRONICLES 29:20

## 2 Chronicles

And all the sons of Israel saw when the fire came down and the glory of the LORD came on the temple, and they bowed their faces low to the ground on the pavement, and they worshipped confessing, "The LORD is good, and His mercy endures forever."

—2 CHRONICLES 7:3

Then they will say, "Because they abandoned the LORD, the God of their fathers who brought them up from the land of Egypt, and they took hold of other gods and worshipped and served them; therefore He has brought on them all this disaster."

—2 CHRONICLES 7:22

Then Jehoshaphat bowed his face to the ground, and all Judah and those dwelling in Jerusalem fell before the LORD to worship Him.

—2 CHRONICLES 20:18

The entire assembly worshipped, the singers sang, and the trumpeters sounded. All of this took place until the burnt offering was finished.

—2 CHRONICLES 29:28

When the burnt offering was finished, the king and all those with him bowed down and worshipped.

—2 CHRONICLES 29:29

Then Hezekiah the king and the officials ordered the Levites to praise the LORD with the words of David and Asaph the seer. So they praised with gladness and bowed down to worship.

—2 CHRONICLES 29:30

Then the sons of Israel present in Jerusalem kept the Feast of Unleavened Bread for seven days with great joy, and the Levites and priests praised the

LORD every day, singing with loud instruments to the LORD.

—2 CHRONICLES 30:21

Has not Hezekiah himself taken down this god's high places and altars by ordering Judah and Jerusalem, "You all will bow down at one altar and on it burn sacrifices"?

—2 CHRONICLES 32:12

And he turned again to build the high places that his father Hezekiah had torn down, and he set up altars to the Baals, and made Asherah poles, and worshipped the starry assembly of heaven and served them.

—2 CHRONICLES 33:3

## Nehemiah

When Ezra blessed the LORD as the great God, all the people responded "Amen, Amen!" By lifting up their hands as they bowed their heads, they worshipped the LORD with their faces to the ground.

—NEHEMIAH 8:6

Then he said to them, "Go your way. Eat the fat, drink the sweet drink, and send portions to those for whom nothing is prepared; for this day is holy to our LORD. Do not be grieved, for the joy of the LORD is your strength."

—NEHEMIAH 8:10

They stood in their place and read from the Book of the Law of the Lord their God for a fourth of the day. And for another fourth, they confessed and worshipped the Lord their God.

—Nehemiah 9:3

## Psalms

But as for me, in the abundance of Your mercy I will enter Your house; in fear of You I will worship at Your holy temple.

—Psalm 5:7

You have made sure that children and infants praise you. Their praise is a wall that stops the talk of your enemies.

—Psalm 8:2, nirv

I will give thanks to You, O Lord, with my whole heart; I will declare all Your marvelous works. I will be glad and rejoice in You; I will sing praise to Your name, O Most High.

—Psalm 9:1–2

Sing praises to the Lord who dwells in Zion; declare His deeds among the people.

—Psalm 9:11

That I may recount all Your praise in the gates of the daughter of Zion, that I may rejoice in Your salvation.

—Psalm 9:14

You will make known to me the path of life; in Your presence is fullness of joy; at Your right hand there are pleasures for evermore.

—Psalm 16:11

I love You, O Lord, my strength.

—Psalm 18:1

I will call on the Lord, who is worthy to be praised, and I will be saved from my enemies.

—Psalm 18:3

Therefore I will give thanks to You, O Lord, among the nations, and sing praises to Your name.

—Psalm 18:49

Be exalted, Lord, by Your strength; may we sing and make music to Your might.

—Psalm 21:13

But You are holy, O You who inhabits the praises of Israel.

—Psalm 22:3

I will declare Your name to my community; in the midst of the congregation I will praise You. You who fear the Lord, praise Him; all you descendants of Jacob, glorify Him, and stand in awe of Him, all you descendants of Israel.

—Psalm 22:22–23

From You my praise will be in the great congregation; I will pay my vows before those who fear Him. The meek will eat and be satisfied; those who seek Him will praise the LORD. May your hearts live forever. All the ends of the world will remember and turn to the LORD, and all the families of the nations will worship before You.

—PSALM 22:25–27

All the prosperous of the earth will eat and worship; all those who go down to the dust (the dead) will bow before Him, even he who cannot keep his soul alive.

—PSALM 22:29, AMP

That I may proclaim with the voice of thanksgiving, and tell of all Your wondrous works.

—PSALM 26:7

One thing I have asked from the LORD, that will I seek after—for me to dwell in the house of the LORD all the days of my life, to see the beauty of the LORD, and to inquire in His temple.

—PSALM 27:4

Now my head will be lifted up above my enemies encircling me; therefore I will offer sacrifices of joy in His tabernacle; I will sing, yes, I will sing praises to the LORD.

—PSALM 27:6

The LORD is my strength and my shield; my heart trusted in Him, and I was helped; therefore my heart rejoices, and with my song I will thank Him.

—PSALM 28:7

Give to the LORD the glory of His name; worship the LORD in holy splendor.

—PSALM 29:2

So that my glory may sing praise to You and not be silent. O LORD my God, I will give thanks to You forever.

—PSALM 30:12

Oh, love the LORD, all you His saints, for the LORD preserves the faithful, but amply repays the one who acts in pride.

—PSALM 31:23

You are my hiding place; You will preserve me from trouble; You will surround me with shouts of deliverance. Selah

—PSALM 32:7

Be glad in the LORD, and rejoice, you righteous one; and shout for joy, all you who are upright in heart!

—PSALM 32:11

Rejoice in the LORD, O you righteous, for praise is fitting for the upright. Give thanks to the LORD with the harp; make music to Him with an instrument of ten strings. Sing to Him a new song; play an instrument skillfully with a joyful shout.

—PSALM 33:1–3

I will bless the LORD at all times; His praise will continually be in my mouth.

—PSALM 34:1

Oh, taste and see that the Lord is good; blessed is the man who takes refuge in Him.

—Psalm 34:8

I will give You thanks in the great congregation; I will praise You among a mighty people.

—Psalm 35:18

My tongue will speak of Your righteousness and of Your praise all the day long.

—Psalm 35:28

He has put a new song in my mouth, even praise to our God; many will see it, and fear, and will trust in the Lord.

—Psalm 40:3

May all those who seek You rejoice and be glad in You; may those who love Your salvation say continually, "The Lord is magnified."

—Psalm 40:16

When I remember these things, I pour out my soul within me. For I would travel with the throng of people; I proceeded with them to the house of God, with the voice of joy and thanks, with a multitude making a pilgrimage. Why are you cast down, O my soul? And why are you disquieted in me? Hope in God, for I will yet thank Him for the help of His presence.

—Psalm 42:4–5

Yet the LORD will command His lovingkindness in the daytime, and in the night His song will be with me, a prayer to the God of my life.

—PSALM 42:8

Then the King will desire your beauty; because He is your LORD, bow down and honor Him.

—PSALM 45:11, AMP

There is a river whose streams make glad the city of God, the holy dwelling place of the Most High.

—PSALM 46:4

Clap your hands, all you people! Shout to God with a joyful voice.

—PSALM 47:1

God went up with a shout, the LORD with the sound of a trumpet.

—PSALM 47:5

May Mount Zion rejoice, may the daughters of Judah be glad, because of Your judgments.

—PSALM 48:11

Out of Zion, the perfection of beauty, God has shined.

—PSALM 50:2

Sacrifice a thank offering to God, and pay your vows to the Most High.

—PSALM 50:14

Be exalted, O God, above the heavens; may Your glory be above all the earth.

—Psalm 57:5

Thus will I bless You while I live; I will lift up my hands in Your name.

—Psalm 63:4

All the earth will worship You and will sing to You; they will sing to Your name." Selah.

—Psalm 66:4

"All the earth will [bow down to] worship You [in submissive wonder], and will sing praises to You; they will praise Your name in song." Selah.

—Psalm 66:4, amp

O let the nations be glad and sing for joy: for thou shalt judge the people righteously, and govern the nations upon earth. Selah.

—Psalm 67:4, kjv

The earth shook; the heavens also poured down rain at the presence of God; even Sinai shook at the presence of God, the God of Israel.

—Psalm 68:8

I will praise the name of God with a song, and will magnify Him with thanksgiving.

—Psalm 69:30

For God will save Zion, and will build the cities of Judah; that they may dwell there, and take possession of it.

—Psalm 69:35

May all kings bow down before him; may all nations serve him.

—Psalm 72:11

Blessed be His glorious name forever; and may the whole earth be filled with His glory. Amen, and Amen.

—Psalm 72:19

We give thanks to You, O God; we give thanks, and Your name is near; Your wondrous works declare it.

—Psalm 75:1

In Judah God is known; in Israel His name is great.

—Psalm 76:1

May I remember my song in the night; may I meditate in my heart; my spirit made a diligent search.

—Psalm 77:6

But chose the tribe of Judah, Mount Zion which He loves.

—Psalm 78:68

There shall be no strange god among you; neither shall you bow down to any strange god.

—Psalm 81:9

All nations whom You have made shall come and worship before You, O Lord, and shall glorify Your name.

—Psalm 86:9

It is good to give thanks to the Lord, and to sing praises unto Your name, O Most High.

—Psalm 92:1

But my horn You have exalted like the horn of the wild ox; You have anointed me with fresh oil.

—Psalm 92:10

O come, let us sing unto the Lord;
    let us make a joyful noise to the rock of
        our salvation!
Let us come before His presence with
    thanksgiving;
    let us make a joyful noise unto Him
        with psalms!
For the Lord is a great God,
    and a great King above all gods.
In His hand are the deep places of the earth;
    the heights of the mountains are also His.
The sea is His, for He made it,
    and His hands formed the dry land.
O come, let us worship and bow down;
    let us kneel before the Lord, our Maker.
For He is our God,
    and we are the people of His pasture
    and the sheep of His hand.

—Psalm 95:1–7

O sing unto the LORD a new song; sing unto the LORD, all the earth!

—PSALM 96:1

Honor and majesty are before Him; strength and beauty are in His sanctuary.

—PSALM 96:6

Worship the LORD in the beauty of holiness; tremble before Him, all the earth.

—PSALM 96:9

All who serve graven images are ashamed, who boast in worthless idols; worship Him, all you gods. Zion hears and is glad, and the daughters of Judah rejoice because of Your judgments, O LORD.

—PSALM 97:7–8

Oh, sing to the LORD a new song, for He has done marvelous deeds! His right hand and His holy arm have accomplished deliverance.

—PSALM 98:1

Exalt the LORD our God, and worship at His footstool—He is holy!

—PSALM 99:5

Exalt the LORD our God, and worship at His holy mountain; for the LORD our God is holy!

—PSALM 99:9

Make a joyful noise unto the LORD, all the earth! Serve the LORD with gladness;
 come before His presence with singing.

Know that the LORD, He is God;

it is He who has made us, and not we ourselves;

we are His people, and the sheep of His pasture.

Enter into His gates with thanksgiving,

and into His courts with praise;

be thankful to Him, and bless His name.

—PSALM 100:1–4

So the nations shall fear the name of the LORD, and all the kings of the earth Your glory.

—PSALM 102:15

Bless the LORD, O my soul, and all that is within me, bless His holy name. Bless the LORD, O my soul, and forget not all His benefits, who forgives all your iniquities, who heals all your diseases.

—PSALM 103:1–3

Praise the LORD! Oh, give thanks unto the LORD, for He is good, for His mercy endures forever.

—PSALM 106:1

They made a calf at Horeb, and worshipped the molded image.

—PSALM 106:19

Save us, O LORD our God, and gather us from among the nations, to give thanks unto Your holy name and to boast in Your praise.

—PSALM 106:47

Oh, give thanks unto the LORD, for He is good, for His mercy endures forever!

—PSALM 107:1

And let them offer the sacrifices of thanksgiving and declare His works with rejoicing.

—PSALM 107:22

When Israel went out of Egypt, the house of Jacob from a people of strange language, Judah was His sanctuary, and Israel His dominion. The sea saw it and fled; the Jordan was driven back.

—PSALM 114:1–3

I will offer to You the sacrifice of thanksgiving and will call upon the name of the LORD.

—PSALM 116:17

The LORD is my strength and song; He has become my salvation.

—PSALM 118:14

At midnight I will rise to give thanks to You, because of Your righteous judgments.

—PSALM 119:62

Then our mouth was filled with laughter, and our tongue with singing. Then they said among the nations, "The LORD has done great things for them."

—PSALM 126:2

We will go to His dwelling place, we will worship at His footstool.

—Psalm 132:7

Let Your priests be clothed with righteousness, and let Your godly ones shout for joy.

—Psalm 132:9

I will also clothe her priests with salvation, and her godly ones shall shout for joy.

—Psalm 132:16

Come, bless the Lord, all you servants of the Lord, who by night stand in the house of the Lord. Lift up your hands in the sanctuary, and bless the Lord.

—Psalm 134:1–2

O give thanks unto the Lord; for he is good:
    for his mercy endureth for ever.
O give thanks unto the God of gods:
    for his mercy endureth for ever.
O give thanks to the Lord of lords:
    for his mercy endureth for ever.
To him who alone doeth great wonders:
    for his mercy endureth for ever.
To him that by wisdom made the heavens:
    for his mercy endureth for ever.
To him that stretched out the earth above
    the waters:
    for his mercy endureth for ever.
To him that made great lights:
    for his mercy endureth for ever:

The sun to rule by day:

 for his mercy endureth for ever:

The moon and stars to rule by night:

 for his mercy endureth for ever.

To him that smote Egypt in their firstborn:

 for his mercy endureth for ever:

And brought out Israel from among them:

 for his mercy endureth for ever:

With a strong hand, and with a stretched out arm:

 for his mercy endureth for ever.

To him which divided the Red sea into parts:

 for his mercy endureth for ever:

And made Israel to pass through the midst of it:

 for his mercy endureth for ever:

But overthrew Pharaoh and his host in the Red sea:

 for his mercy endureth for ever.

To him which led his people through the wilderness:

 for his mercy endureth for ever.

To him which smote great kings:

 for his mercy endureth for ever:

And slew famous kings:

 for his mercy endureth for ever:

Sihon king of the Amorites:

 for his mercy endureth for ever:

And Og the king of Bashan:

 for his mercy endureth for ever:

And gave their land for an heritage:

 for his mercy endureth for ever:

Even an heritage unto Israel his servant:

 for his mercy endureth for ever.

Who remembered us in our low estate:
    for his mercy endureth for ever:
And hath redeemed us from our enemies:
    for his mercy endureth for ever.
Who giveth food to all flesh:
    for his mercy endureth for ever.
O give thanks unto the God of heaven:
    for his mercy endureth for ever.

—PSALM 136:1–26, KJV

I will bow down [in worship] toward Your holy temple and give thanks to Your name for Your lovingkindness and Your truth; for You have magnified Your word together with Your name.

—PSALM 138:2, AMP

Let my prayer be set forth before You as incense, and the lifting up of my hands as the evening sacrifice.

—PSALM 141:2

I will sing a new song unto You, O God, on a harp and an instrument of ten strings I will sing praises unto You.

—PSALM 144:9

He sends out His word and melts them; He causes His wind to blow and the waters flow.

—PSALM 147:18

Let them praise the name of the LORD, for His name alone is excellent; His glory is above the earth and heaven.

—PSALM 148:13

Praise the LORD! Sing unto the LORD a new song, and His praise in the assembly of the godly ones.

—PSALM 149:1

Praise the LORD!
Praise God in His sanctuary;
    praise Him in the firmament of His power!
Praise Him for His mighty acts;
    praise Him according to His excellent greatness!
Praise Him with the sound of the trumpet;
    praise Him with the lyre and harp!
Praise Him with the tambourine and dancing;
    praise Him with stringed instruments and flute!
Praise Him with loud cymbals;
    praise Him with the clanging cymbals!
Let everything that has breath praise the LORD.
Praise the LORD!

—PSALM 150

## Isaiah

In that day a man shall cast away his idols of silver and his idols of gold, which they made for themselves to worship, to the moles and to the bats.

—ISAIAH 2:20

And in that day you shall say: O Lord, I will praise You; though You were angry with me, Your anger has turned away, and You comforted me.

—Isaiah 12:1

In that day you shall say: Praise the Lord, call upon His name, declare His deeds among the peoples, make them remember that His name is exalted.

—Isaiah 12:4

O Lord, You are my God. I will exalt You, I will praise Your name, for You have done wonderful things; Your plans formed of old are faithfulness and truth.

—Isaiah 25:1

And in that day the great trumpet shall be blown, and those who were ready to perish in the land of Assyria and the outcasts in the land of Egypt shall worship the Lord in the holy mount at Jerusalem.

—Isaiah 27:13

In that day the Lord of Hosts shall become a crown of glory and a diadem of beauty to the remnant of His people.

—Isaiah 28:5

It shall blossom abundantly and rejoice even with joy and singing. The glory of Lebanon shall be given to it, the excellency of Carmel and Sharon. They shall see the glory of the Lord and the excellency of our God.

—Isaiah 35:2

And the ransomed of the LORD shall return and come to Zion with songs and everlasting joy upon their heads. They shall obtain joy and gladness, and sorrow and sighing shall flee away.

—ISAIAH 35:10

Sing to the LORD a new song, and His praise from the ends of the earth, you who go down to the sea, and all that is in it, the coastlands, and the inhabitants.

—ISAIAH 42:10

Let them give glory to the LORD, and declare His praise in the islands.

—ISAIAH 42:12

This people I have formed for Myself; they shall declare My praise.

—ISAIAH 43:21

Sing, O heavens, for the LORD has done it. Shout joyfully, you lower parts of the earth; break forth into singing, you mountains, O forest, and every tree in it. For the LORD has redeemed Jacob, and glorified Himself in Israel.

—ISAIAH 44:23

Thus says the LORD, the Redeemer of Israel, and his Holy One, to the despised one, to the one whom the nation abhors, to the servant of rulers: "Kings shall see and arise, princes also shall worship,

because of the Lord who is faithful and the Holy
One of Israel who has chosen you."

—Isaiah 49:7

Sing, O heavens! And be joyful, O earth! And break
forth into singing, O mountains! For the Lord has
comforted His people and will have mercy on His
afflicted.

—Isaiah 49:13

For the Lord shall comfort Zion, He will comfort all her waste places; He will make her wilderness like Eden, and her desert like the garden of the
Lord; joy and gladness shall be found in it, thanksgiving, and the voice of melody.

—Isaiah 51:3

Therefore, the redeemed of the Lord shall return
and come with singing to Zion, and everlasting joy
shall be upon their head. They shall obtain gladness
and joy, and sorrow and mourning shall flee away.

—Isaiah 51:11

Sing, O barren, you who did not bear a child. Break
forth into singing and cry aloud, you who did not
travail with child. For more are the children of the
desolate than the children of the married wife, says
the Lord.

—Isaiah 54:1

For you shall go out with joy, and be led out with
peace; the mountains and the hills shall break forth

into singing before you, and all the trees of the field shall clap their hands.

—Isaiah 55:12

The multitude of camels shall cover your land, the young camels of Midian and Ephah; all those from Sheba shall come; they shall bring gold and incense and shall bear good news of the praises of the Lord.

—Isaiah 60:6

Violence shall no more be heard in your land, nor devastation or destruction within your borders; but you shall call your walls Salvation and your gates Praise.

—Isaiah 60:18

To preserve those who mourn in Zion, to give to them beauty for ashes, the oil of joy for mourning, the garment of praise for the spirit of heaviness, that they might be called trees of righteousness, the planting of the Lord, that He might be glorified.

—Isaiah 61:3

I will greatly rejoice in the Lord, my soul shall be joyful in my God; for He has clothed me with the garments of salvation, He has covered me with the robe of righteousness, as a bridegroom decks himself with ornaments, and as a bride adorns herself with her jewels. For as the earth brings forth her buds, and as the garden causes the things that are sown in it to spring forth, so the Lord God will cause righteousness and praise to spring forth before all the nations.

—Isaiah 61:10–11

I will mention the steadfast love of the Lord and the praises of the Lord, according to all that the Lord has bestowed on us, and the great goodness toward the house of Israel, which He has bestowed on them according to His mercy, and according to the multitude of His kindnesses.

—Isaiah 63:7

I will bring forth descendants from Jacob, and out of Judah an inheritor of My mountains; and My chosen ones shall inherit it, and My servants shall dwell there.

—Isaiah 65:9

From one New Moon to another, and from one Sabbath to another, all flesh shall come to worship before Me, says the Lord.

—Isaiah 66:23

## Jeremiah

This evil people, who refuse to hear My words, who walk in the imagination of their hearts, and walk after other gods, to serve them, and to worship them, shall be even as this waistband which is good for nothing.

—Jeremiah 13:10

And do not go after other gods to serve them and to worship them, and provoke Me not to anger with the works of your hands; and I will do you no harm.

—JEREMIAH 25:6

The women also said, "When we burned incense to the queen of heaven, and poured out drink offerings to her, did we make her cakes to worship her and pour out drink offerings to her without our husbands?"

—JEREMIAH 44:19

## Ezekiel

He brought me into the inner court of the house of the LORD, and at the door of the temple of the LORD, between the porch and the altar, were about twenty-five men with their backs toward the temple of the LORD and their faces toward the east. And they worshipped the sun toward the east.

—EZEKIEL 8:16

Then I will make their waters settle, and cause their rivers to run like oil, says the Lord GOD.

—EZEKIEL 32:14

It was according to the appearance of the vision which I saw, even according to the vision that I saw, when He came to destroy the city. And the visions were like the vision that I saw by the River Kebar. And I fell upon my face. The glory of the LORD came into the temple by the way of the gate facing east. So the Spirit took me up and brought me into the inner court. And the glory of the Lord filled the temple. Then I heard one speaking to me out of the temple. And a man stood by me.

—Ezekiel 43:3–6

## Daniel

Then King Nebuchadnezzar fell upon his face and did homage to Daniel, and commanded that they should present an offering and sweet incense to him.

—Daniel 2:46

That at the time you hear the sound of the cornet, flute, harp, sackbut, psaltery, dulcimer, and all kinds of music, you should fall down and worship the golden image that Nebuchadnezzar the king has set up.

—Daniel 3:5

And whoever does not fall down and worship shall the same hour be cast into the midst of a burning fiery furnace.

—Daniel 3:6

Therefore at that time, when all the people heard the sound of the cornet, flute, harp, sackbut, psaltery, and all kinds of music, all the peoples, the nations, and the languages fell down and worshipped the golden image that Nebuchadnezzar the king had set up.

—Daniel 3:7

You, O king, have made a decree, that every man who hears the sound of the cornet, flute, harp, sackbut, psaltery, and dulcimer, and all kinds of music should fall down and worship the golden image.

—Daniel 3:10

And whoever does not fall down and worship should be cast into the midst of a burning fiery furnace.

—Daniel 3:11

There are certain Jews whom you have set over the affairs of the province of Babylon: Shadrach, Meshach, and Abednego. These men, O king, have not regarded you. They do not serve your gods or worship the golden image which you have set up.

—Daniel 3:12

Nebuchadnezzar spoke and said to them, "Is it true, Shadrach, Meshach, and Abednego, that you do not serve my gods or worship the golden image which I have set up?"

—Daniel 3:14

Now if you are ready at the time you hear the sound of the cornet, flute, harp, sackbut, psaltery, and dulcimer, and all kinds of music to fall down and worship the image which I have made, very well. But if you do not worship, you shall be cast the same hour into the midst of a burning fiery furnace. And who is that god who can deliver you out of my hands?

—Daniel 3:15

If it be so, our God whom we serve is able to deliver us from the burning fiery furnace, and He will deliver us out of your hand, O king. But even if He does not, be it known to you, O king, that we will not serve your gods, nor worship the golden image which you have set up.

—Daniel 3:17–18

Then Nebuchadnezzar spoke and said, "Blessed be the God of Shadrach, Meshach, and Abednego, who has sent His angel and delivered His servants who trusted in Him. They have defied the king's word, and yielded their bodies, that they might not serve nor worship any god, except their own God."

—Daniel 3:28

## Joel

You will eat abundantly and be satisfied, and you will praise the name of the Lord your God, who has worked wonders for you; and My people will never again be shamed.

—Joel 2:26

And it will be that in that day the mountains will drip sweet wine, and the hills will flow with milk, and all the streambeds of Judah will flow with water; a spring will proceed from the house of the Lord and will water the Valley of Shittim.

—Joel 3:18

## Micah

Then I will cut off your idols, and your sacred stones from among you, and you will no longer bow down to the work of your hands.

—MICAH 5:13

## Habakkuk

For the earth will be filled with the knowledge of the glory of the LORD, as the waters cover the seas.

—HABAKKUK 2:14

## Zephaniah

The LORD will be dreadful to them, for He will weaken all the gods of the earth; men will worship Him, every one from his place, all the lands of the nations.

—ZEPHANIAH 2:11

## Zechariah

Then it will be that all the nations who have come against Jerusalem and survived will go up each year to worship the King, the LORD of Hosts, and to celebrate the Feast of Tabernacles. And it will happen that if any of the families of the earth do not go up to Jerusalem to worship the King, the LORD of Hosts, then there will not be rain for them.

—ZECHARIAH 14:16–17

## 3

# WORSHIP IN THE NEW TESTAMENT

In the New Testament the ability to worship God is extended outside the Israelite priesthood to all who come to believe in Christ. Christ fulfilled the requirements of the Law through His death by becoming the ultimate sin sacrifice. There was no need for animal sacrifices in the New Testament, so worship became a privilege and a spiritual way to express gratitude to God for giving His Son as a payment for our sin.

First Peter 2:5 says that we, "as a holy priesthood," are "to offer up spiritual sacrifices that are acceptable to God through Jesus Christ." As will be seen in the verses that follow, spiritual sacrifices of worship include submitting ourselves to God (Rom. 12:1), praise (Heb. 13:15), financial or material giving (Phil. 4:18), and serving others (Heb. 13:16).

The New Testament was mostly written in Greek, and the following words that refer to the types of new covenant worship are seen repeatedly throughout the New Testament:

- *Proskyneō*—appears in fifty-four verses in the New Testament (first instance, Matthew 2:2) and refers to "kneeling or prostration to do homage (to one) or make obeisance, whether in order to express respect or to make supplication."[1]

- *Sebō*—appears ten times in the New Testament (first instance, Matthew 15:9) and means "to revere, to worship."[2]

- *Eusebeō*—appears only once in the New Testament (Acts 17:23) and means "to act piously or reverently towards God, one's country, magistrates, relations, and all to whom dutiful regard or reverence is due."[3]

- *Ethelothrēskia*—appears only once in the New Testament (Col. 2:23) and means "voluntary, arbitrary worship"; "worship which one prescribes and devises for himself, contrary to the contents and nature of faith which ought to be directed to Christ."[4]

- *Latreuō*—appears twenty-one times in the New Testament (first instance, Matthew 4:10), and it means "to render religious service or homage, to worship"; "to perform sacred services, to offer gifts, to worship God in the observance of the rites instituted for his worship of priests, to officiate, to discharge the sacred office."[5]

- *Piptō*—appears with the following meaning two times in the New Testament (Matt. 4:9; Rev. 4:10). The complete definition of the word with this usage is "to descend from an erect to a prostrate position"; "to fall down"; "to be prostrated, fall prostrate"; "to prostrate one's self"; "used of suppliants and persons rendering homage or worship to one."[6]

Let's now look at these words in action.

## Matthew

Where is He who was born King of the Jews? For we have seen His star in the east and have come to worship Him.

—Matthew 2:2

And when they came into the house, they saw the young Child with Mary, His mother, and fell down and worshipped Him. And when they had opened their treasures, they presented gifts to Him: gold, frankincense, and myrrh.

—Matthew 2:11

And [the devil] said to Him, "All these things I will give You if You will fall down and worship me." Then Jesus said to him, "Get away from here, Satan! For it is written, 'You shall worship the Lord your God, and Him only shall you serve.'"

—Matthew 4:9–10

And then a leper came and worshipped Him, saying, "Lord, if You are willing, You can make me clean."

—Matthew 8:2

Neither do men put new wine into old wineskins. Or else the wineskins burst, the wine runs out, and the wineskins perish. But they put new wine into new wineskins, and both are preserved.

—Matthew 9:17

While He was speaking these things to them, a certain ruler came and worshipped Him, saying, "My daughter is even now dead. But come and lay Your hand on her, and she will live."

—Matthew 9:18

Then those who were in the boat came and worshipped Him, saying, "Truly You are the Son of God."

—Matthew 14:33

In vain they do worship Me, teaching as doctrines the precepts of men.

—Matthew 15:9

Then she came and worshipped Him, saying, "Lord, help me."

—Matthew 15:25

Then the mother of Zebedee's sons came to Him with her sons. And kneeling before Him, she asked for a certain thing.

—Matthew 20:20

The crowds that went before Him and that followed Him cried out: "Hosanna to the Son of David! 'Blessed is He who comes in the name of the Lord!' Hosanna in the highest!"

—Matthew 21:9

But when the chief priests and the scribes saw the wonderful and miraculous things that Jesus had done, and heard the boys who were shouting in [the porticoes and courts of] the temple [in praise and adoration], "Hosanna to the Son of David (the Messiah)," they became indignant.

—Matthew 21:15, amp

And said to Him, "Do You hear what these are saying?" Jesus said to them, "Yes. Have you never read, 'Out of the mouth of children and infants You have perfected praise'?"

—Matthew 21:16

As they went to tell His disciples, suddenly Jesus met them, saying, "Greetings!" They came and took hold of His feet and worshipped Him.

—Matthew 28:9

When they saw Him, they worshipped Him. But some doubted.

—MATTHEW 28:17

## Mark

And no one pours new wine into old wineskins, or else the new wine bursts the wineskins, and the wine is spilled, and the wineskins will be marred. But new wine must be poured into new wineskins.

—MARK 2:22

But when he saw Jesus afar off, he ran up and kneeled before Him.

—MARK 5:6

In vain do they worship Me, teaching as doctrines the precepts of men.

—MARK 7:7

## Luke

And no one puts new wine into old wineskins. Otherwise the new wine will burst the wineskins, and it will be spilled, and the wineskins will be destroyed. But new wine must be put into new wineskins, and both are preserved. And no one, having drunk old wine, immediately desires new. For he says, "The old is better."

—LUKE 5:37–39

Then they worshipped Him, and returned to Jerusalem with great joy.

—Luke 24:52

## John

"Our fathers worshipped on this mountain, but you all say that in Jerusalem is the place where men ought to worship."

Jesus said to her, "Woman, believe Me, the hour is coming when neither on this mountain nor in Jerusalem will you worship the Father. You worship what you do not know; we know what we worship, for salvation is of the Jews. Yet the hour is coming, and is now here, when the true worshippers will worship the Father in spirit and truth. For the Father seeks such to worship Him. God is Spirit, and those who worship Him must worship Him in spirit and truth."

—John 4:20–24

He who believes in Me, as the Scripture has said, out of his heart shall flow rivers of living water.

—John 7:38

Then he said, "Lord, I believe." And he worshipped Him.

—John 9:38

Now there were some Greeks among those who went up to worship at the feast.

—John 12:20

## Acts

But God turned and gave them up to worship the host of heaven, as it is written in the book of the Prophets: "O House of Israel, have you offered to Me slain animals and sacrifices for forty years in the wilderness?"

—Acts 7:42

So he rose up and went. And there was a man of Ethiopia, a eunuch of great authority under Candace, queen of the Ethiopians, who was in command of her entire treasury. He had come to Jerusalem to worship.

—Acts 8:27

A woman named Lydia, a seller of purple fabric of the city of Thyatira, who worshipped God, heard us. The Lord opened her heart to acknowledge what Paul said.

—Acts 16:14

For as I passed by and looked up at your objects of worship, I found an altar with this inscription: To the Unknown God. Whom you therefore unknowingly worship, Him I proclaim to you.

—Acts 17:23

Nor is He served by men's hands, as though He needed anything, since He gives all men life and breath and all things.

—Acts 17:25

Then he departed from there and entered the house of a man named Justus, one who worshipped God, whose house was next door to the synagogue.

—Acts 18:7

Saying, "This man is persuading men to worship God contrary to the law."

—Acts 18:13

Now not only is our trade in danger of coming into disrepute, but also the temple of the great goddess Artemis, whom all Asia and the world worship, may be discredited and her magnificence destroyed.

—Acts 19:27

However, I affirm that in accordance with the Way, which they call a sect, I worship the God of my fathers and believe everything written in the Law and in the Prophets.

—Acts 24:14

## Romans

They turned the truth of God into a lie and worshipped and served the creature rather than the Creator, who is blessed forever. Amen.

—Romans 1:25

For the kingdom of God does not mean eating and drinking, but righteousness and peace and joy in the Holy Spirit.

—Romans 14:17

## 1 Corinthians

But if all prophesy and there comes in one who does not believe or one unlearned, he is convinced by all and judged by all. Thus the secrets of his heart are revealed. And so falling down on his face, he will worship God and report that God is truly among you.

—1 Corinthians 14:24–25

## 2 Corinthians

Blessed be God, the Father of our Lord Jesus Christ, the Father of mercies, and the God of all comfort.

—2 Corinthians 1:3

## Ephesians

Do not be drunk with wine, for that is reckless living. But be filled with the Spirit. Speak to one another in psalms, hymns, and spiritual songs, singing and making melody in your heart to the Lord. Give thanks always for all things to God the Father in the name of our Lord Jesus Christ.

—Ephesians 5:18–20

## Philippians

For we are the circumcision who worship God in the Spirit, and boast in Christ Jesus, and place no trust in the flesh.

—Philippians 3:3

## Colossians

Let the word of Christ dwell in you richly in all wisdom, teaching and admonishing one another in psalms and hymns and spiritual songs, singing with grace in your hearts to the Lord.

—COLOSSIANS 3:16

## Hebrews

Saying: "I will declare Your name to My brothers; in the midst of the congregation I will sing praise to You."

—HEBREWS 2:12

Through Him, then, let us continually offer to God the sacrifice of praise, which is the fruit of our lips, giving thanks to His name.

—HEBREWS 13:15

## 1 Peter

Blessed [gratefully praised and adored] be the God and Father of our Lord Jesus Christ, who according to His abundant and boundless mercy has caused us to be born again [that is, to be reborn from above—spiritually transformed, renewed, and set apart for His purpose] to an ever-living hope and confident assurance through the resurrection of Jesus Christ from the dead.

—1 PETER 1:3, AMP

But you are a chosen race, a royal priesthood, a holy nation, a people for God's own possession, so that you may declare the goodness of Him who has called you out of darkness into His marvelous light.

—1 Peter 2:9

If anyone speaks, let him speak as the oracles of God. If anyone serves, let him serve with the strength that God supplies, so that God in all things may be glorified through Jesus Christ, to whom be praise and dominion forever and ever. Amen.

—1 Peter 4:11

## Revelation

The twenty-four elders fall down before Him who sits on the throne, and worship Him, who lives forever and ever. Then they cast their crowns before the throne.

—Revelation 4:10

And they sang a new song, saying: "You are worthy to take the scroll, and to open its seals; for You were slain, and have redeemed us to God by Your blood out of every tribe and tongue and people and nation."

—Revelation 5:9

The four living creatures said, "Amen." And the twenty-four elders fell down and worshipped Him who lives forever and ever.

—Revelation 5:14

All the angels stood around the throne and the elders and the four living creatures and fell on their faces before the throne and worshipped God.

—Revelation 7:11

The rest of mankind, who were not killed by these plagues, did not repent of the works of their hands. They did not cease to worship demons, and idols of gold, silver, brass, stone, and wood, which cannot see nor hear nor walk.

—Revelation 9:20

They sang a new song before the throne and before the four living creatures and the elders. No one could learn that song except the one hundred and forty-four thousand who were redeemed from the earth.

—Revelation 14:3

He said with a loud voice, "Fear God and give Him glory, for the hour of His judgment has come. Worship Him who made heaven and earth, the sea and the springs of water."

—Revelation 14:7

Who shall not fear You, O Lord, and glorify Your name? For You alone are holy. All nations shall come and worship before You, for Your judgments have been revealed.

—Revelation 15:4

The twenty-four elders and the four living creatures fell down and worshipped God who sat on the throne, saying: "Amen! Alleluia!" Then a voice came from the throne, saying: "Praise our God, all you His servants and those who fear Him, both small and great!"

—Revelation 19:4–5

I fell at his feet to worship him. But he said to me, "See that you not do that. I am your fellow servant, and of your brothers who hold the testimony of Jesus. Worship God! For the testimony of Jesus is the spirit of prophecy."

—Revelation 19:10

I, John, am he who saw and heard these things. When I heard and saw them, I fell down to worship at the feet of the angel who showed me these things. But he said to me, "See that you not do that. For I am your fellow servant, and of your brothers the prophets, and of those who keep the words of this book. Worship God!"

—Revelation 22:8–9

# PART II

# HOLINESS
## SCRIPTURES

# 4

# BE HOLY AS I AM HOLY

Holiness is a major theme of the Scriptures. The numerous references to holiness found in the Bible reveal that it is an important aspect of the life of the believer. In this section we are going to look at the subject of holiness in a way that will help you meditate and have revelation on what holiness is and how to please God by being holy. First Peter 1:14–16 says:

> As obedient children do not conduct yourselves according to the former lusts in your ignorance. But as He who has called you is holy, so be holy in all your conduct, because it is written, "Be holy, for I am holy."

*Holiness* is "the quality or state of being holy."[1] *Holy* means "exalted or worthy of complete devotion as one perfect in goodness and righteousness"; "divine."[2] It also means "specially recognized as or declared sacred by religious use or authority; consecrated: holy ground;

dedicated or devoted to the service of God, the church, or religion: a holy man; saintly; godly; pious; devout: a holy life; having a spiritually pure quality."[3] The opposite of holiness is defilement, corruption, uncleanness, iniquity, filthiness, and impurity.

God is holy. Zion, the mountain of God, is holy. Jesus is the holy one of God (Mark 1:24). The Old Testament priests were called to be holy, and God's servants are called to be holy. God's people are called the holy ones—saints (Ps. 16:3; 1 Thess. 3:13). We worship in the beauty of holiness. God speaks in His holiness, and the Word of God exhorts us to live holy lives. Our ability to be called saints is connected with our desire to please God through our actions and conduct. We cannot fully please the Lord without holiness.

As I mentioned before, by beholding the beauty, glory, and holiness of the Lord, we become changed, consecrated, sanctified, and set apart. By meditating on His holiness through the revelation of His Word, we are renewed into greater realms of faith, glory, and holiness.

Again, the scriptures included in this section show examples and instances of holy living as well as manifestations of the opposite. The key verses for this section are:

> Consecrate yourselves therefore, and be holy, for I am the LORD your God.
> —LEVITICUS 20:7

Pursue peace with all men, and the holiness without which no one will see the Lord.

—HEBREWS 12:14

# 5

# HOLINESS IN THE OLD TESTAMENT

*oly* is the Hebrew word *qodesh*. In the Old Testament, it is translated most commonly as "holy" but also as "sanctuary," holy or hallowed things, "holiness," "dedicated," "hallowed," and "consecrated."[1] *Qodesh* means "apartness, holiness, sacredness, separateness" and the "apartness, sacredness, holiness of God, of places, of things"; "set-apartness, separateness."[2] This word is derived from another Hebrew word, *qadash*, which is translated as "sanctify, hallow, dedicate, holy, prepare, consecrate, appointed, bid, purified," and means "to consecrate, sanctify, prepare, dedicate, be hallowed, be holy, be sanctified, be separate."[3]

In this chapter we are going to look at how this definition of holiness is expressed in the Old Testament.

## Genesis

If you do well, shall you not be accepted? But if you do not do well, sin is crouching at the door. It desires to dominate you, but you must rule over it.

—GENESIS 4:7

The earth was corrupt before God and filled with violence. God looked on the earth and saw it was corrupt, for all flesh had corrupted their way on the earth.

—GENESIS 6:11–12

The LORD said to Noah, "You and your entire household go into the ark, for you alone I have seen to be righteous before Me among this generation."

—GENESIS 7:1

Abram believed the LORD, and He credited it to him as righteousness.

—GENESIS 15:6

Then Abraham drew near and said, "Shall You also destroy the righteous with the wicked? What if there are fifty righteous in the city? Shall You also destroy, and not spare the place, for the fifty righteous who are in it? Far be it from You to do such a thing as this, to slay the righteous with the wicked, so that the righteous should be treated like the wicked; far be it from You. Should not the Judge of all the earth do right?"

So the LORD said, "If I find in Sodom fifty

righteous within the city, then I will spare the entire place for their sakes."

—Genesis 18:23–26

"Suppose there were five less than the fifty righteous. Will You destroy all the city for lack of five?" And He said, "If I find forty-five there, I will not destroy it."

—Genesis 18:28

There is none greater in this house than I. He has kept nothing back from me but you, because you are his wife. How then can I do this great wickedness and sin against God?

—Genesis 39:9

## Exodus

He said, "Do not approach here. Remove your sandals from off your feet, for the place on which you are standing is holy ground."

—Exodus 3:5

Who is like You, O Lord, among the gods? Who is like You, glorious in holiness, fearful in praises, doing wonders?

—Exodus 15:11

In Your mercy You have led the people whom You have redeemed; You have guided them by Your strength to Your holy dwelling.

—Exodus 15:13

"And you will be to Me a kingdom of priests and a holy nation." These are the words which you shall speak to the children of Israel.

—Exodus 19:6

The Lord said to Moses, "Indeed, I am going to come to you in a thick cloud, so that the people may hear when I speak with you and always believe in you." Then Moses told the words of the people to the Lord.

The Lord said to Moses, "Go to the people and sanctify them today and tomorrow, and have them wash their clothes, and be ready for the third day, for on the third day the Lord will come down in the sight of all the people on Mount Sinai."

—Exodus 19:9–11

So Moses went down from the mountain to the people and sanctified the people, and they washed their clothes.

—Exodus 19:14

Let the priests also, which come near to the Lord, sanctify themselves, lest the Lord break through against them.

—Exodus 19:22

You will be holy men to Me; therefore you must not eat any flesh that is torn by beasts in the field. You must throw it to the dogs.

—Exodus 22:31

You shall make holy garments for your brother Aaron, for glory and for beauty.

—Exodus 28:2

You shall make a plate of pure gold and engrave on it, like the engravings of a signet, holiness to the Lord.

—Exodus 28:36–37

You shall put them on Aaron your brother, and on his sons with him, and shall anoint them, and consecrate them, and sanctify them, that they may minister to Me as priests.

—Exodus 28:41

And you shall put the turban on his head and put the holy crown on the turban.

—Exodus 29:6

I will sanctify the tent of meeting and the altar. I will also sanctify both Aaron and his sons to minister as priests to Me.

—Exodus 29:44

And you must make with it a holy anointing oil, a perfumed compound, the work of a perfumer. It will be a holy anointing oil.

—Exodus 30:25

You must speak to the children of Israel, saying, "This will be a holy anointing oil to Me throughout your generations."

—Exodus 30:31

The LORD spoke to Moses, "Go, and get down, for your people, whom you brought out of the land of Egypt, have corrupted themselves."

—Exodus 32:7

He made the holy anointing oil and the pure incense of sweet spices, according to the work of a perfumer.

—Exodus 37:29

They made the plate of the holy crown of pure gold and wrote on it an inscription, like the engravings of a signet: holiness to the Lord.

—Exodus 39:30

You shall put the holy garments on Aaron and anoint him and consecrate him, so that he may minister to Me as a priest.

—Exodus 40:13

## Leviticus

So that you may differentiate between what is holy and common and between what is unclean and clean.

—Leviticus 10:10

For I am the LORD your God. You shall therefore sanctify yourselves, and you shall be holy, for I am holy. Neither shall you defile yourselves with any manner of crawling thing that moves on the ground. For I am the LORD who brings you up out of the land of Egypt to be your God. Therefore you shall be holy, for I am holy.

—Leviticus 11:44–45

For on that day the priest shall make atonement for you to cleanse you, so that you may be clean from all your sins before the Lord.

—Leviticus 16:30

Do not defile yourselves in any of these ways, for in these practices the nations I am casting out before you have defiled themselves. And the land has become defiled; therefore I have punished its iniquity, and the land has vomited out her inhabitants.

—Leviticus 18:24–25

Lest the land vomit you out also when you defile it, as it vomited out the nations that were before you.

—Leviticus 18:28

Therefore you shall keep My ordinances, that you do not commit any one of these abominable customs which were committed before you, so that you do not defile yourselves by them: I am the Lord your God.

—Leviticus 18:30

Speak to all the congregation of the children of Israel, and say to them: You shall be holy, for I the Lord your God am holy.

—Leviticus 19:2

Do not turn to spirits through mediums or necromancers. Do not seek after them to be defiled by them: I am the LORD your God.

—LEVITICUS 19:31

I will set My face against that man and will cut him off from among his people, because he has given some of his descendants to Molech to defile My sanctuary and to defile My holy name.

—LEVITICUS 20:3

Consecrate yourselves therefore, and be holy, for I am the LORD your God. You shall keep My statutes, and do them; I am the LORD who sanctifies you.

—LEVITICUS 20:7–8

You shall be holy unto Me; for I the LORD am holy and have separated you from other peoples, that you should be Mine.

—LEVITICUS 20:26

You shall not defile My holy name, but I will be sanctified among the children of Israel: I am the LORD who sanctifies you.

—LEVITICUS 22:32

For it is the Jubilee. It shall be holy to you. You shall eat the produce of the field.

—LEVITICUS 25:12

Any tithe of the land, whether seed of the land or fruit of the trees, belongs to the Lord. It is holy to the Lord.

—Leviticus 27:30

# Numbers

And the Lord spoke to Moses, saying: Speak to the children of Israel and say to them: When either a man or woman will make a hard vow, the vow of a Nazirite, to separate themselves to the Lord, he will separate himself from wine and strong drink and will drink no vinegar of wine, or vinegar of strong drink. Neither shall he drink any juice of grapes, nor eat fresh or dry grapes.

—Numbers 6:1–3

# Deuteronomy

For you are a holy people to the Lord your God. The Lord your God has chosen you to be His special people, treasured above all peoples who are on the face of the earth.

—Deuteronomy 7:6

For you are a holy people to the Lord your God, and the Lord has chosen you to be a peculiar people to Himself, treasured above all the nations that are on the earth.

—Deuteronomy 14:2

When you enter into the land which the LORD your God gives you, you must not learn to practice the abominations of those nations.

—DEUTERONOMY 18:9

For all that do these things are an abomination to the LORD, and because of these abominations the LORD your God will drive them out from before you.

—DEUTERONOMY 18:12

For the LORD your God walks in the midst of your camp, to deliver you, and to defeat your enemies before you. Therefore, your camp must be holy, so that He does not see any indecent thing among you, and turn away from you.

—DEUTERONOMY 23:14

Look down from Your holy habitation, from heaven, and bless Your people Israel and the land which You have given us, as You swore to our fathers, a land flowing with milk and honey.

—DEUTERONOMY 26:15

He will exalt you above all nations which He has made, in praise, and in name, and in honor; and that you may be a holy people to the LORD your God, just as He has spoken.

—DEUTERONOMY 26:19

The LORD will establish you as a holy people to Himself, just as He swore to you, if you will keep the commandments of the LORD your God and walk in His ways.

—DEUTERONOMY 28:9

They have acted corruptly to Him; they are not His children, but blemished; they are a perverse and crooked generation.

—DEUTERONOMY 32:5

The LORD came from Sinai and rose up from Seir to them; He shone forth from Mount Paran, and He came with ten thousands of holy ones; from His right hand went a fiery law for them.

Surely, He loved the people; all His holy ones are in Your hand, and they sit down at Your feet; everyone receives Your words.

—DEUTERONOMY 33:2–3

## Joshua

Joshua said to the people, "Consecrate yourselves, for tomorrow the LORD will perform wondrous deeds among you."

—JOSHUA 3:5

Get up! Consecrate the people and say, "Consecrate yourselves for tomorrow, for thus says the LORD, the God of Israel: 'Things dedicated for destruction are in your midst, O Israel. You are not able to stand before your enemies until you remove the things dedicated for destruction from your midst.'"

—JOSHUA 7:13

Then Joshua said to the people, "You are not able to serve the LORD, for He is a holy God. He is a jealous God, and He will not forgive your transgressions nor your sins."

—JOSHUA 24:19

## Judges

For you will conceive and bear a son. No razor may touch his head, for the boy will be a Nazirite to God from the womb. He will begin to save Israel from the hand of the Philistines.

—JUDGES 13:5

He said to me, "You will conceive and bear a son. So now, do not drink wine or strong drink, and do not eat anything ritually unclean, for the boy will be a Nazirite to God from the womb until the day he dies."

—JUDGES 13:7

So he told her all his secrets and said to her, "No razor has touched my head, for I have been a Nazirite to God from my mother's womb. If I were shaven, my strength would leave me, and I would become weak and be like all other men."

—JUDGES 16:17

# 1 Samuel

There is none holy as the LORD, for there is none besides You, and there is no rock like our God.

—1 Samuel 2:2

And he said, "I have come in peace to sacrifice to the LORD. Consecrate yourselves, and come with me to the sacrifice." And he consecrated Jesse and his sons and called them to the sacrifice.

—1 Samuel 16:5

# 1 Kings

The priests and Levites brought up the ark of the LORD, the tabernacle of the congregation, and all the holy implements that were in the tabernacle.

—1 Kings 8:4

Solomon offered a sacrifice of peace offerings, which he offered to the LORD, twenty-two thousand oxen and a hundred and twenty thousand sheep. So the king and all the children of Israel dedicated the house of the LORD.

—1 Kings 8:63

There were also male cult prostitutes in the land, and they did according to all the abominations of the nations that the LORD cast out before the children of Israel.

—1 Kings 14:24

## 2 Kings

And she said to her husband, "I know that he is a holy man of God regularly passing through near us."

—2 KINGS 4:9

Moreover, Josiah disposed of the mediums, the soothsayers, the teraphim, the idols, and all the abominations that were seen in the land of Judah and in Jerusalem, so that he established the words of the law that were written in the book that Hilkiah the priest found in the house of the LORD.

—2 KINGS 23:24

## 1 Chronicles

He said to them, "You are the captains of the fathers' houses for the Levites. Consecrate yourselves, you and your brothers, so you may bring up the ark of the LORD, the God of Israel, to the place I have prepared for it."

—1 CHRONICLES 15:12

Glory in His holy name; let the heart of those who seek the LORD rejoice.

—1 CHRONICLES 16:10

Give to the LORD the glory due His name; bring an offering and come before Him, bow down to the LORD in holy array.

—1 CHRONICLES 16:29

Now say, "Save us, O God of our salvation, and gather us and deliver us from the nations, that we may give thanks to Your holy name, to glory in Your praise."

—1 Chronicles 16:35

The sons of Amram were Aaron and Moses, but Aaron was set apart to consecrate the most holy things, he and his sons forever, to offer sacrifices before the Lord, to minister to Him, and to bless in His name forever.

—1 Chronicles 23:13

And that they should keep charge of the tent of meeting and the sanctuary and attend to the sons of Aaron, their brothers, for the service of the house of the Lord.

—1 Chronicles 23:32

Moreover, in my devotion to the house of my God I have offered from my own property, gold and silver, which I give for the house of my God, over and above that which I prepared for the holy dwelling place.

—1 Chronicles 29:3

O Lord our God, all this abundance that we have prepared to build You a house for Your holy name has come from Your hand, and all belongs to You.

—1 Chronicles 29:16

## 2 Chronicles

Now rise up, O Lord God, to Your resting place, both You and the ark of Your strength. And let Your priests, O Lord God, be clothed in salvation and Your loyal ones rejoice in goodness.

—2 Chronicles 6:41

He brought into the house of God the sacred gifts of his father and his own sacred gifts—silver, gold, and utensils.

—2 Chronicles 15:18

And he consulted with the people and then appointed singers for the Lord and those praising Him in holy attire as they went before those equipped for battle saying, "Praise the Lord, for His mercy endures forever."

—2 Chronicles 20:21

Listen to me, Levites. Consecrate yourselves and consecrate the house of the Lord God of your fathers. And bring out the detestable things from the holy sanctuary.

—2 Chronicles 29:5

However there were too few priests, and they were not able to skin the burnt offerings. But their brothers the Levites helped them until the work was finished and more priests consecrated themselves,

for the Levites were more upright in heart to consecrate themselves than the priests.

—2 CHRONICLES 29:34

For there were many in the assembly who had consecrated themselves, so the Levites slaughtered the
Passover lamb for those who were not clean in order
to consecrate the people to the LORD.

—2 CHRONICLES 30:17

They were registered with all their little children,
wives, sons, and daughters for the entire assembly
for they consecrated themselves in faithfulness.

—2 CHRONICLES 31:18

And in the eighth year of his reign, while he was
still a young boy, he began to seek out the God of
David his father; and in the twelfth year he began
to cleanse Judah and Jerusalem from high places,
Asherah poles, idols, and carved and cast images.

—2 CHRONICLES 34:3

Then slaughter the Passover lamb and consecrate
yourselves and prepare for your brothers to do
according to the word of the LORD by the hand
of Moses.

—2 CHRONICLES 35:6

## Ezra

Then they ate together, both the children of Israel
who had come out of captivity and all those who

had separated themselves from the uncleanness of the nations of the land, in order to seek the LORD God of Israel.

—EZRA 6:21

You are holy to the LORD. The vessels are holy also. The silver and the gold are a freewill offering to the LORD God of your fathers.

—EZRA 8:28

The land you are going to possess, it is an unclean land with the filthiness of the people of the lands. By their abominations, it is has been filled from one end to another with their uncleanness.

—EZRA 9:11

## Nehemiah

Then I commanded the Levites to purify themselves so that they could come and, as guardians of the gates, sanctify the Sabbath day. Remember me, O my God, concerning this also, and spare me according to Your abundant mercy.

—NEHEMIAH 13:22

## Psalms

Blessed is the man
    who walks not in the counsel of the ungodly,
nor stands in the path of sinners,
    nor sits in the seat of scoffers;
but his delight is in the law of the LORD,

and in His law he meditates day and night.
He will be like a tree planted by the rivers of water,
    that brings forth its fruit in its season;
its leaf will not wither,
    and whatever he does will prosper.
The ungodly are not so,
    but are like the chaff
    which the wind drives away.
Therefore the ungodly will not stand in the
    judgment,
nor sinners in the congregation of the righteous.
For the Lord knows the way of the righteous,
    but the ways of the ungodly will perish.

—Psalm 1:1–6

I have installed My king on Zion, My holy hill.
—Psalm 2:6

I cried to the Lord with my voice, and He answered
me from His holy hill. Selah.
—Psalm 3:4

Know that the Lord set apart the faithful for
Himself; the Lord hears when I call to Him.
—Psalm 4:3

But as for me, in the abundance of Your mercy I
will enter Your house; in fear of You I will worship
at Your holy temple.
—Psalm 5:7

For You, LORD, will bless the righteous; You surround him with favor like a shield.

—PSALM 5:12

The LORD is in His holy temple, His throne is in heaven; His eyes see, His eyes examine mankind.

—PSALM 11:4

Help, LORD, for the godly man comes to an end, for the faithful disappear from sons of men.

—PSALM 12:1

The words of the LORD are pure words; they are silver tried in an earthen furnace refined seven times.

—PSALM 12:6

LORD, who will abide in Your tabernacle?
Who will dwell in Your holy hill?
He who walks uprightly,
    and does righteousness,
and speaks truth in his heart;
he who does not slander with the tongue
    and does no evil to his neighbor,
    nor bears a reproach against his friend;
in whose eyes a vile person is despised,
    but who honors those who fear the LORD;
he who swears to avoid evil
    and does not change;
he who does not put his money out to usury,
    nor take a bribe against the innocent.

He who does these things
  will never be moved.

—Psalm 15:1–5

For the holy ones who are in the land, they are the majestic ones; in them is all my delight.

—Psalm 16:3

The Lord rewarded me according to my righteousness; according to the cleanness of my hands He has repaid me.

—Psalm 18:20

Therefore the Lord has repaid me according to my righteousness, according to the cleanness of my hands in His view.

—Psalm 18:24

With the pure You will show Yourself pure; and with the crooked You will show Yourself crooked.

—Psalm 18:26

The fear of the Lord is clean, enduring forever; the judgments of the Lord are true and righteous altogether.

—Psalm 19:9

But You are holy, O You who inhabits the praises of Israel.

—Psalm 22:3

Who may ascend the hill of the Lord?
  Who may stand in His holy place?
He who has clean hands and a pure heart;

who has not lifted up his soul unto vanity,
nor sworn deceitfully.

—PSALM 24:3–4

Hear the voice of my supplications when I cry to You, when I lift up my hands toward Your most holy place.

—PSALM 28:2

Give to the LORD the glory of His name; worship the Lord in holy splendor.

—PSALM 29:2

Ascribe to the LORD the glory due His name; Worship the LORD in the beauty and majesty of His holiness [as the creator and source of holiness].

—PSALM 29:2, AMP

Sing to the LORD, O you saints of His, and give thanks at the remembrance of His holiness.

—PSALM 30:4

Oh, love the LORD, all you His saints, for the LORD preserves the faithful, but amply repays the one who acts in pride.

—PSALM 31:23

For this cause everyone who is godly will pray to You in a time when You may be found; surely in the floods of great waters they will not reach him.

—PSALM 32:6

Oh, fear the Lord, you His saints; for the ones who fear Him will not be in need.

—Psalm 34:9

For the Lord loves justice, and does not forsake His saints; they are preserved forever, but the descendants of the wicked will be cut off.

—Psalm 37:28

When I remember these things, I pour out my soul within me. For I would travel with the throng of people; I proceeded with them to the house of God, with the voice of joy and thanks, with a multitude making a pilgrimage.

—Psalm 42:4

Send out Your light and Your truth. Let them lead me; let them bring me to Your holy hill, and to Your dwelling place.

—Psalm 43:3

There is a river whose streams make glad the city of God, the holy dwelling place of the Most High.

—Psalm 46:4

God reigns over the nations; God sits on His holy throne.

—Psalm 47:8

Great is the Lord, and greatly to be praised in the city of our God, in His holy mountain.

—Psalm 48:1

Gather My faithful ones together to Me, those who have made a covenant with Me by sacrifice.

—Psalm 50:5

Wash me thoroughly from my iniquity, and cleanse me from my sin.

—Psalm 51:2

Purify me with hyssop, and I will be clean; wash me, and I will be whiter than snow.

—Psalm 51:7

Create in me a clean heart, O God, and renew a right spirit within me.

—Psalm 51:10

Do not cast me away from Your presence, and do not take Your Holy Spirit from me.

—Psalm 51:11

God has spoken in His holiness: "I will rejoice, I will divide Shechem, and measure out the Valley of Sukkoth."

—Psalm 60:6

Blessed is the man You choose and allow to draw near; he will dwell in Your courts. We will be satisfied with the goodness of Your house, even of Your holy temple.

—Psalm 65:4

A father of the fatherless, and a protector of the widows, is God in His holy habitation.

—Psalm 68:5

The chariots of God are myriads, thousands upon thousands; The Lord is among them as He was at Sinai, in holiness.

—Psalm 68:17, amp

They have seen Your [solemn] procession, O God, The procession of my God, my King, into the sanctuary [in holiness].

—Psalm 68:24, amp

O God, You are awesome from Your sanctuaries; the God of Israel is He who gives strength and power to people. Blessed be God!

—Psalm 68:35

I will give You thanks with the harp, even Your truth, O my God; to You I will sing with the lyre, O Holy One of Israel.

—Psalm 71:22

Truly God is good to Israel, to the pure in heart.

—Psalm 73:1

Yes, they tested God over and over, and provoked the Holy One of Israel.

—Psalm 78:41

O God, the nations have come into Your inheritance; Your holy temple they have defiled; they have laid Jerusalem in ruins.

—Psalm 79:1

Help us, O God of our salvation, for the glory of Your name; deliver us, and purge away our sins, for Your name's sake.

—Psalm 79:9

Preserve my soul, for I am godly; You are my God; save Your servant who trusts in You.

—Psalm 86:2

The city of His foundation is on the holy mountain.

—Psalm 87:1

Let the heavens praise Your wonders, O Lord; Your faithfulness also in the assembly of the holy ones.

—Psalm 89:5

God is greatly to be feared in the assembly of the holy ones and awesome to all those who surround Him.

—Psalm 89:7

For the Lord is our shield of defense, and the Holy One of Israel is our king.

—Psalm 89:18

Long ago You spoke in a vision to Your godly one and said: "I have given help to one who is mighty; I have exalted one chosen from the people."

—Psalm 89:19

I have found David, My servant; with My holy oil I have anointed him.

—Psalm 89:20

Your statutes are very sure; holiness is becoming to Your house, O Lord, forever.

—Psalm 93:5

Worship the Lord in the beauty of holiness; tremble before Him, all the earth.

—Psalm 96:9

You who love the Lord, hate evil! He preserves the lives of His devoted ones; He delivers them from the hand of the wicked.

—Psalm 97:10

Rejoice in the Lord, you righteous, and give thanks at the memory of His holy name.

—Psalm 97:12

Oh, sing to the Lord a new song, for He has done marvelous deeds! His right hand and His holy arm have accomplished deliverance.

—Psalm 98:1

Let them praise Your great and awesome name—He is holy!

—Psalm 99:3

Exalt the Lord our God, and worship at His footstool—He is holy!

—Psalm 99:5

Exalt the Lord our God, and worship at His holy mountain; for the Lord our God is holy!

—Psalm 99:9

Bless the LORD, O my soul, and all that is within me, bless His holy name.

—PSALM 103:1

Glory in His holy name; let the heart rejoice for those who seek the LORD.

—PSALM 105:3

For he recalled His holy promise to Abraham His servant.

—PSALM 105:42

Save us, O LORD our God, and gather us from among the nations, to give thanks unto Your holy name and to boast in Your praise.

—PSALM 106:47

Your people will follow you in the day of your battle; on the holy mountains at dawn of the morning, the dew of your youth belongs to you.

—PSALM 110:3

He sent redemption to His people; He has commanded His covenant forever; holy and fearful is His name.

—PSALM 111:9

Praise the LORD!
Blessed is the man who fears the LORD,
    who delights greatly in His commandments.
His offspring shall be mighty in the land;
    the generation of the upright shall be blessed.

Wealth and riches shall be in his house,
and his righteousness endures forever.

—Psalm 112:1–3

Precious in the sight of the Lord is the death of
His godly ones.

—Psalm 116:15

Blessed are those whose way is blameless, who walk
in the law of the Lord.

—Psalm 119:1

How shall a young man keep his way pure? By
keeping it according to Your word.

—Psalm 119:9

Your word I have hidden in my heart, that I might
not sin against You.

—Psalm 119:11

Let Your priests be clothed with righteousness, and
let Your godly ones shout for joy.

—Psalm 132:9

I will also clothe her priests with salvation, and her
godly ones shall shout for joy.

—Psalm 132:16

I will worship toward Your holy temple, and praise
Your name for Your lovingkindness and for Your
truth; for You have exalted Your word above all
Your name.

—Psalm 138:2

Search me, O God, and know my heart; try me, and know my concerns, and see if there is any rebellious way in me, and lead me in the ancient way.

—Psalm 139:23–24

The Lord is righteous in all His ways and loving in all His works.

—Psalm 145:17

My mouth shall speak the praise of the Lord, and let all people bless His holy name forever and ever.

—Psalm 145:21

He has raised up a victory horn for His people, praise for all His saints, even for the people of Israel near Him. Praise the Lord!

—Psalm 148:14

Praise the Lord! Sing unto the Lord a new song, and His praise in the assembly of the godly ones.

—Psalm 149:1

Let the godly ones be joyful in glory; let them sing for joy on their beds.

—Psalm 149:5

## Proverbs

The fear of the Lord is the beginning of knowledge, but fools despise wisdom and instruction.

—Proverbs 1:7

He keeps the paths of justice, and preserves the way of His saints.

—Proverbs 2:8

Keep your heart with all diligence, for out of it are the issues of life.

—Proverbs 4:23

These six things the Lord hates,
yes, seven are an abomination to him:
    a proud look,
    a lying tongue,
    and hands that shed innocent blood,
    a heart that devises wicked imaginations,
    feet that are swift in running to mischief,
    a false witness who speaks lies,
    and he who sows discord among brethren.

—Proverbs 6:16–19

The fear of the Lord is to hate evil; pride and arrogance and the evil way and the perverse mouth I hate.

—Proverbs 8:13

The fear of the Lord is the beginning of wisdom, and the knowledge of the Holy One is understanding.

—Proverbs 9:10

The fear of the Lord prolongs days, but the years of the wicked will be shortened.

—Proverbs 10:27

A hypocrite with his mouth destroys his neighbor, but through knowledge the just will be delivered.

—Proverbs 11:9

Fools make a mock at sin, but among the righteous there is favor.

—Proverbs 14:9

The fear of the Lord is a fountain of life, to depart from the snares of death.

—Proverbs 14:27

It is a snare to the man who dedicates rashly that which is holy, and after the vows to make inquiry.

—Proverbs 20:25

Do not let your heart envy sinners, but continue in the fear of the Lord all day long.

—Proverbs 23:17

I neither learned wisdom, nor have the knowledge of the holy.

—Proverbs 30:3

There is a generation that is pure in its own eyes, and yet is not washed from its filthiness.

—Proverbs 30:12

## Song of Songs

I slept, but my heart was awake. A sound! My beloved is knocking. "Open to me, my sister, and my love, my dove, my perfect one; for my head is wet with dew, my locks with the drops of the night."

—SONG OF SONGS 5:2

## Isaiah

Alas, sinful nation, a people laden with iniquity, a brood of evildoers, children who deal corruptly! They have forsaken the LORD, they have provoked the Holy One of Israel to anger, they are estranged and backward.

—ISAIAH 1:4

Wash yourselves, make yourselves clean; put away the evil from your deeds, from before My eyes. Cease to do evil.

—ISAIAH 1:16

And I will turn My hand against you, thoroughly purge away your dross, and take away all your impurities.

—ISAIAH 1:25

He who is left in Zion and he who remains in Jerusalem shall be called holy, even everyone who is written among the living in Jerusalem. When the Lord has washed away the filth of the daughters of Zion and has purged the blood of Jerusalem from the midst by the spirit of justice and by the spirit of burning...

—ISAIAH 4:3–4

But the LORD of Hosts shall be exalted in judgment, and God who is holy shall be hallowed in righteousness.

—ISAIAH 5:16

But the LORD of hosts will be exalted in justice, And God, the Holy One, will show Himself holy in righteousness [through His righteous judgments].

—ISAIAH 5:16, AMP

One cried to another and said: "Holy, holy, holy, is the LORD of Hosts; the whole earth is full of His glory."

—ISAIAH 6:3

And he laid it on my mouth, and said, "This has touched your lips, and your iniquity is taken away, and your sin purged."

—ISAIAH 6:7

It is the LORD of hosts whom you are to regard as holy and awesome. He shall be your [source of] fear, He shall be your [source of] dread [not man].

—ISAIAH 8:13, AMP

In that day the remnant of Israel and those who have escaped of the house of Jacob shall never again depend on him who struck them, but shall depend on the LORD, the Holy One of Israel, in truth.

—ISAIAH 10:20

They shall not hurt or destroy in all My holy mountain, for the earth shall be full of the knowledge of the LORD, as the waters cover the sea.

—ISAIAH 11:9

Cry out and shout for joy, O inhabitant of Zion. For great is the Holy One of Israel in your midst.

—ISAIAH 12:6

On that day a man shall look to his Maker, and his eyes shall have respect for the Holy One of Israel.

—ISAIAH 17:7

And in that day the great trumpet shall be blown, and those who were ready to perish in the land of Assyria and the outcasts in the land of Egypt shall worship the LORD in the holy mount at Jerusalem.

—ISAIAH 27:13

The meek also shall increase their joy in the LORD, and the poor among men shall rejoice in the Holy One of Israel.

—ISAIAH 29:19

But when he sees his children, the work of My hands, in his midst, they shall sanctify My name and sanctify the Holy One of Jacob, and fear the God of Israel.

—ISAIAH 29:23

For thus says the Lord GOD, the Holy One of Israel: In returning and rest you shall be saved; in quietness and in confidence shall be your strength. Yet you were not willing.

—Isaiah 30:15

You shall have songs, as in the night when a festival is kept, and gladness of heart, as when one goes with a flute to come into the mountain of the Lord, to the Mighty One of Israel.

—Isaiah 30:29

The sinners in Zion are afraid; fearfulness has seized the hypocrites: "Who among us can live with the continual fire? Who among us can live with everlasting burning?"

—Isaiah 33:14

A highway shall be there, a roadway, and it shall be called the Highway of Holiness. The unclean shall not pass on it, but it shall be for the wayfaring men, and fools shall not wander on it.

—Isaiah 35:8

To whom then will you liken Me, that I should be equal to him? says the Holy One.

—Isaiah 40:25

Do not fear, you worm Jacob, and you men of Israel. I will help you, says the Lord and your Redeemer, the Holy One of Israel.

—Isaiah 41:14

You shall fan them, and the wind shall carry them away, and the whirlwind shall scatter them; and you shall rejoice in the LORD, and shall glory in the Holy One of Israel.

—Isaiah 41:16

That they may see, and know, and consider, and understand together, that the hand of the LORD has done this, and the Holy One of Israel has created it.

—Isaiah 41:20

For I am the LORD your God, the Holy One of Israel, your Savior; I gave Egypt for your ransom, Ethiopia and Seba in your place.

—Isaiah 43:3

Thus says the LORD, your Redeemer, the Holy One of Israel: For your sake I have sent to Babylon, and have brought down all their nobles, and the Chaldeans, into the ships in which they rejoice.

—Isaiah 43:14

I am the LORD, your Holy One, the Creator of Israel, your King.

—Isaiah 43:15

Thus says the LORD, the Holy One of Israel and his Maker: Ask Me of things to come concerning My sons, and you shall commit to Me the work of My hands.

—Isaiah 45:11

As for our Redeemer, the LORD of Hosts is His name, the Holy One of Israel.

—Isaiah 47:4

For they call themselves after the holy city, and lean on the God of Israel; the Lord of Hosts is His name.

—Isaiah 48:2

Thus says the Lord, your Redeemer, the Holy One of Israel: I am the Lord your God, who teaches you to profit, who leads you in the way you should go.

—Isaiah 48:17

Thus says the Lord, the Redeemer of Israel, and his Holy One, to the despised one, to the one whom the nation abhors, to the servant of rulers: "Kings shall see and arise, princes also shall worship, because of the Lord who is faithful and the Holy One of Israel who has chosen you."

—Isaiah 49:7

Awake, awake! Put on your strength, O Zion; put on your beautiful garments, O Jerusalem, the holy city. For the uncircumcised and the unclean will no longer enter you.

—Isaiah 52:1

The Lord has bared His holy arm in the eyes of all the nations, and all the ends of the earth shall see the salvation of our God.

—Isaiah 52:10

Depart, depart, go out from there, touch no unclean thing; go out of the midst of her; be clean, you who bear the vessels of the Lord.

—Isaiah 52:11

For your Maker is your husband, the LORD of Hosts is His name; and your Redeemer is the Holy One of Israel; He shall be called the God of the whole earth.

—Isaiah 54:5

Surely you shall call a nation that you do not know, and nations that did not know you shall run to you because of the LORD your God, even the Holy One of Israel; for He has glorified you.

—Isaiah 55:5

Even them I will bring to My holy mountain and make them joyful in My house of prayer. Their burnt offerings and their sacrifices shall be accepted on My altar; for My house shall be called a house of prayer for all people.

—Isaiah 56:7

When you cry out, let your collection of idols deliver you. But the wind shall carry them all away, a breath shall take them away. But he who puts his trust in Me shall possess the land and shall inherit My holy mountain.

—Isaiah 57:13

For thus says the High and Lofty One who inhabits eternity, whose name is Holy: I dwell in the high and holy place and also with him who is of a contrite and humble spirit, to revive the spirit of the humble, and to revive the heart of the contrite ones.

—Isaiah 57:15

If because of the Sabbath you turn away your foot from doing your pleasure on My holy day, and call the Sabbath a delight, the holy day of the LORD honorable, and honor it, not doing your own ways, nor finding your own pleasure, nor speaking your own words, then you shall delight yourself in the LORD, and I will cause you to ride upon the high places of the earth.

—ISAIAH 58:13–14

Surely the coastlands shall wait for Me, and the ships of Tarshish shall come first, to bring your sons from afar, their silver and their gold with them, to the name of the LORD your God and to the Holy One of Israel because He has glorified you.

—ISAIAH 60:9

The sons also of those who afflicted you shall come bowing before you, and all those who despised you shall bow themselves down at the soles of your feet; and they shall call you, The City of the LORD, the Zion of the Holy One of Israel.

—ISAIAH 60:14

I will greatly rejoice in the LORD, my soul shall be joyful in my God; for He has clothed me with the garments of salvation, He has covered me with the robe of righteousness, as a bridegroom decks himself with ornaments, and as a bride adorns herself with her jewels.

—ISAIAH 61:10

They shall call them The Holy People, the Redeemed of the LORD; and you shall be called Sought Out, a City Not Forsaken.

—ISAIAH 62:12

But they rebelled and grieved His Holy Spirit; therefore, He turned Himself to be their enemy, and He fought against them.

—ISAIAH 63:10

Look down from heaven and see, from Your holy and glorious habitation. Where are Your zeal and Your strength? The stirrings of Your heart and Your mercies toward me are restrained.

—ISAIAH 63:15

But you are those who forsake the LORD, who forget My holy mountain, who prepare a table for Fortune, and who furnish the drink offering for Destiny.

—ISAIAH 65:11

The wolf and the lamb shall feed together, and the lion shall eat straw like the bull, and dust shall be the serpent's food. They shall not hurt nor destroy in all My holy mountain, says the LORD.

—ISAIAH 65:25

They shall bring all your brothers out of all nations as an offering to the LORD on horses, and in chariots, and in litters, and on mules, and on swift beasts to My holy mountain Jerusalem, says the

LORD, as the sons of Israel bring an offering in a clean vessel into the house of the LORD.

—ISAIAH 66:20

## Jeremiah

Israel is holy to the LORD, and the first fruits of His harvest. All who eat of it will become guilty; disaster will come upon them, says the LORD.

—JEREMIAH 2:3

Therefore thus says the LORD: If you return, then I will bring you back, and you shall stand before Me; and if you take out the precious from the worthless, you will be My spokesman. Let them return to you, but do not return to them.

—JEREMIAH 15:19

My heart is broken within me, because of the prophets; all my bones shake; I am like a drunken man, like a man overcome by wine, because of the LORD, and because of His holy words.

—JEREMIAH 23:9

Therefore prophesy against them all these words, and say to them: The LORD will roar from on high, and utter His voice from His holy habitation; He will mightily roar against His fold. He will give a shout, as those who tread the grapes, against all the inhabitants of the earth.

—JEREMIAH 25:30

Thus says the LORD of Hosts, the God of Israel: Once again they shall use this speech in the land of Judah and in the cities when I restore their fortunes: "May the LORD bless you, O habitation of righteousness and mountain of holiness!"

—JEREMIAH 31:23

## Lamentations

Her princes were purer than snow, whiter than milk; their bodies were more ruddy than rubies, their appearance like sapphire.

—LAMENTATIONS 4:7

## Ezekiel

And I will purge from among you the rebels and those who transgress against Me. I will bring them out of the country where they sojourn, and they shall not enter into the land of Israel. And you shall know that I am the LORD.

—EZEKIEL 20:38

For on My holy mountain, on the mountain of the height of Israel, says the Lord GOD, there all the house of Israel, all of them, shall serve Me in the land. There I will accept them, and there I will seek your offerings and the first fruits of your gifts with all your holy things.

—EZEKIEL 20:40

You have despised My holy things and have profaned My Sabbaths.

—Ezekiel 22:8

Her priests have violated My law and have profaned
My holy things. They have made no distinction
between the holy and profane, nor have they shown
the difference between the unclean and the clean,
and they have hidden their eyes from My Sabbaths,
and I am profaned among them.

—Ezekiel 22:26

In your filthiness is lewdness. Because I would have
purged you, yet you are not purged, you shall not
be purged from your filthiness anymore until I have
caused My fury to rest on you.

—Ezekiel 24:13

When they entered the nations, where they went,
they profaned My holy name, because they said of
them, "These are the people of the Lord and have
gone out of His land."

—Ezekiel 36:20

I will vindicate the sanctity of My great name
which was profaned among the nations, which you
have profaned in their midst. Then the nations shall
know that I am the Lord, says the Lord God, when
I shall be sanctified among you before their eyes.

—Ezekiel 36:23

The nations shall know that I the Lord do sanctify Israel when My sanctuary is in their midst forevermore.

—Ezekiel 37:28

So I will make My holy name known in the midst of My people Israel. And I will not let them pollute My holy name anymore. And the nations shall know that I am the Lord, the Holy One in Israel.

—Ezekiel 39:7

Therefore thus says the Lord God: Now I will restore the fortunes of Jacob and have mercy on the whole house of Israel and will be jealous for My holy name.

—Ezekiel 39:25

When the priests enter it, then they shall not go out of the holy place into the outer court, but there they shall lay their garments in which they minister, for they are holy. And they shall put on other garments, and shall approach those things which are for the people.

—Ezekiel 42:14

He said to me: Son of man, this is the place of My throne and the place of the soles of My feet, where I will dwell in the midst of the sons of Israel forever. And My holy name shall the house of Israel defile no more, nor they nor their kings by their harlotry, nor by the corpses of their kings when they die.

—Ezekiel 43:7

They shall teach My people the difference between the holy and profane, and cause them to discern between the unclean and the clean.

—Ezekiel 44:23

Then he said to me, "This is the place where the priests shall boil the guilt offering and the sin offering, and where they shall bake the grain offering so that they not bear them out into the outer court, to sanctify the people."

—Ezekiel 46:20

## Daniel

But Daniel purposed in his heart that he would not defile himself with the portion of the king's food, nor with the wine which he drank. Therefore he requested of the master of the officials that he might not defile himself.

—Daniel 1:8

But at the last Daniel came in before me, whose name was Belteshazzar according to the name of my god and in whom is the Spirit of the Holy God, and before him I told the dream, saying, "Belteshazzar, master of the magicians, because I know that the Spirit of the Holy God is in you and no secret troubles you, tell me the visions of my dream that I have seen, and its interpretation."

—Daniel 4:8–9

But the saints of the Most High shall take the kingdom and possess the kingdom forever, even forever and ever.

—Daniel 7:18

Until the Ancient of Days came, and judgment was passed in favor of the saints of the Most High, and the time came when the saints possessed the kingdom.

—Daniel 7:22

O Lord, according to all Your righteousness, I beseech You, let Your anger and Your fury be turned away from Your city Jerusalem, Your holy mountain, because for our sins and for the iniquities of our fathers, Jerusalem and Your people have become a reproach to all who are around us.

—Daniel 9:16

While I was speaking and praying and confessing my sin and the sin of my people Israel, and presenting my supplication before the Lord my God for the holy mountain of my God…the man Gabriel…touched me…informed me and talked with me.

—Daniel 9:20–22

Seventy weeks have been determined for your people and upon your holy city, to finish the transgression, and to make an end of sins, and to make atonement for iniquity, and to bring in everlasting righteousness, and to seal up the vision and prophecy, and to anoint the Most Holy Place.

—DANIEL 9:24

And I heard the man clothed in linen, who was over the water of the river, when he held up his right hand and his left hand to heaven, and swore by Him who lives forever that it would be for a time, times, and half a time. And when they finish shattering the power of the holy people, all these things shall be finished.

—DANIEL 12:7

Many shall be purified and made white and tried. But the wicked shall do wickedly, and none of the wicked shall understand, but the wise shall understand.

—DANIEL 12:10

## Joel

Blow the ram's horn in Zion, sound the alarm on My holy mountain! All the inhabitants of the earth will tremble, because the day of the LORD has come, because it is near.

—JOEL 2:1

Gather the people, consecrate the congregation, assemble the elders, gather the children and those nursing at the breast; let the bridegroom leave his room and the bride her chamber.

—JOEL 2:16

Then you will know that I am the Lord your God, who dwells in Zion, My holy mountain. And Jerusalem will be holy, and invaders will never again pass through her.

—Joel 3:17

## Amos

I raised up some of your sons as prophets, and some of your young men as Nazirites. Is it not so, O children of Israel? says the Lord.

—Amos 2:11

Hate evil and love good, and establish justice at the gate. It may then be that the Lord God of Hosts will be gracious to the remnant of Joseph.

—Amos 5:15

## Obadiah

But on Mount Zion there shall be deliverance, and it shall be holy; and the house of Jacob shall possess those who dispossessed them.

—Obadiah 17

## Jonah

Then I said, "I am cast away from Your sight; yet I will look again to Your holy temple."

—Jonah 2:4

When my life was ebbing away, I remembered the LORD; and my prayer came to You, into Your holy temple.

—JONAH 2:7

## Micah

He has told you, O man, what is good—and what does the LORD require of you, but to do justice and to love kindness, and to walk humbly with your God?

—MICAH 6:8

## Habakkuk

Look, his soul is lifted up; it is not upright in him; but the just shall live by his faith.

—HABAKKUK 2:4

But the LORD is in His holy temple. Let all the earth keep silence before Him.

—HABAKKUK 2:20

God came from Teman, and the Holy One from Mount Paran. Selah. His glory covered the heavens, and the earth was full of His praise.

—HABAKKUK 3:3

# Zechariah

And the LORD will possess Judah as His portion in the holy land, and He will again choose Jerusalem.

—ZECHARIAH 2:12

Be still, all flesh before the LORD, for He is stirred from His holy habitation.

—ZECHARIAH 2:13

And the LORD said to Satan, "The LORD rebuke you, Satan! The LORD who has chosen Jerusalem rebukes you! Is this not a burning brand taken out of the fire?"

Now Joshua had on filthy garments and was standing before the angel. And he said to those standing before him, "Take off his filthy garments."

Then he said, "See that I have removed from you your iniquity, and I will clothe you with rich robes."

—ZECHARIAH 3:2–4

Thus says the LORD: I have returned to Zion and will dwell in the midst of Jerusalem, and Jerusalem will be called a city of faithfulness and the mountain of the LORD of Hosts, the holy mountain.

—ZECHARIAH 8:3

On that day "Holy to the Lord" will be engraved on the bells of the horses. And the pots in the house of the LORD will be as the basins before the altar.

—ZECHARIAH 14:20

And every pot in Jerusalem and Judah will be holy to the LORD of Hosts so that all who come to sacrifice will take from those pots and boil the meat in them. And on that day there will no longer be a Canaanite in the house of the LORD of Hosts.

—ZECHARIAH 14:21

## Malachi

But you profane it, in that you say, "The table of the LORD is defiled, and its fruit, that is, its food is contemptible."

—MALACHI 1:12

Judah has dealt treacherously, and an abomination has been committed in Israel and Jerusalem. For Judah has profaned the sanctuary of the LORD, which He loves, and has married the daughter of a foreign god.

—MALACHI 2:11

Yet you say, "Why?" It is because the LORD has been a witness between you and the wife of your youth, against whom you have dealt treacherously. Yet she is your companion and your wife by covenant.

Did He not make them one, having a remnant of the Spirit? And why one? He seeks godly offspring. So take heed to your spirit, that you do not deal treacherously.

For the LORD, the God of Israel, says that He hates divorce; for it covers one's garment with violence, says the LORD of Hosts.

Therefore take heed to your spirit, that you do not deal treacherously.

—Malachi 2:14–16

He will sit as a refiner and purifier of silver; he will purify the sons of Levi, and refine them like gold and silver, and they will present to the Lord offerings in righteousness.

—Malachi 3:3

# 6

# HOLINESS IN THE NEW TESTAMENT

Even though we are in a new covenant with God, God still has a standard of holiness for His people. In comparing the related words and usage of the words *holy* and *holiness* from the Old Testament to the New Testament, we will find that the words maintain consistent application. The benefit of being a new covenant believer is that we have a Helper—the Holy Spirit. He teaches us all things and empowers us by God's grace to walk righteously before the Lord. Instead of fear driving us to obey God, love for Him inspires us to obey Him. Through Jesus, we have come to understand God the Father and His love for us. There is no fear in love.

The Greek word for holy is *hagios*. In the New Testament it is translated as "holy," "saints," "Holy One."[1] It means "sacred"; "something set apart," "special"; "likeness of nature with the Lord," "different from the world."[2]

Being in God's holy presence moves us to repentance. By His holiness, we are pruned and shaped to bear fruit and to be fruitful. His holiness purges us of every unclean thing. We are sanctified and are called the holy ones. Becoming holy as God is holy allows us into His presence. Corruption, defilement, fornication, and iniquity will separate us from the presence of God. God has made a way for us to become holy through the blood of Jesus and the power of the Holy Spirit. He has moved heaven and earth to be with us.

> Therefore, "Come out from among them and be separate, says the LORD. Do not touch what is unclean, and I will receive you. I will be a Father to you, and you shall be My sons and daughters, says the Lord Almighty."
>
> —2 CORINTHIANS 6:17–18

## Matthew

> Therefore, bear fruit worthy of repentance.
>
> —MATTHEW 3:8

> Even now the axe is put to the tree roots. Therefore, every tree which does not bear good fruit is cut down and thrown into the fire.
>
> —MATTHEW 3:10

His fan is in His hand, and He will thoroughly clean His floor and gather His wheat into the granary, but He will burn up the chaff with unquenchable fire.

—MATTHEW 3:12

You are the salt of the earth. But if the salt loses its saltiness, how shall it be made salty? It is from then on good for nothing but to be thrown out and to be trampled underfoot by men.

You are the light of the world. A city that is set on a hill cannot be hidden. Neither do men light a candle and put it under a basket, but on a candlestick. And it gives light to all who are in the house. Let your light so shine before men that they may see your good works and glorify your Father who is in heaven.

—MATTHEW 5:13–16

Therefore, when you do your charitable deeds, do not sound a trumpet before you as the hypocrites do in the synagogues and in the streets, that they may be honored by men. Truly I say to you, they have their reward.

—MATTHEW 6:2

When you pray, you shall not be like the hypocrites. For they love to pray standing in the synagogues and on the street corners that they may be seen by men. Truly I say to you, they have their reward.

—MATTHEW 6:5

Moreover, when you fast, do not be like the hypocrites with a sad countenance. For they disfigure their faces so they may appear to men to be fasting. Truly I say to you, they have their reward.

—Matthew 6:16

You hypocrite! First take the plank out of your own eye, and then you will see clearly to take the speck out of your brother's eye.

—Matthew 7:5

Do not give what is holy to the dogs, nor throw your pearls before swine, lest they trample them under their feet and turn around and attack you.

—Matthew 7:6

You will know them by their fruit. Do men gather grapes from thorns, or figs from thistles? Even so, every good tree bears good fruit. But a corrupt tree bears evil fruit. A good tree cannot bear evil fruit, nor can a corrupt tree bear good fruit.

—Matthew 7:16–18

Therefore, by their fruit you will know them.

—Matthew 7:20

Either make the tree good and its fruit good, or else make the tree corrupt and its fruit corrupt. For the tree is known by its fruit.

—Matthew 12:33

That which goes into the mouth does not defile a man, but that which comes out of the mouth, this defiles a man.

—Matthew 15:11

But those things which proceed out of the mouth come from the heart, and they defile the man.

—Matthew 15:18

These are the things which defile a man. But to eat with unwashed hands does not defile a man.

—Matthew 15:20

Therefore I tell you, the kingdom of God will be taken from you and given to a nation bearing its fruits.

—Matthew 21:43

## Mark

And he cried out, "Leave us alone! What do You have to do with us, Jesus of Nazareth? Have You come to destroy us? I know who You are, the Holy One of God."

—Mark 1:24

And He said, "What comes out of a man is what defiles a man. For from within, out of the heart of men, proceed evil thoughts, adultery, fornication, murder, theft, covetousness, wickedness, deceit, licentiousness, an evil eye, blasphemy, pride and foolishness. All these evil things come from within and defile a man."

—MARK 7:20–23

## Luke

For He who is mighty has done great things for me, and holy is His name.

—LUKE 1:49

To grant us that we, being delivered out of the hand of our enemies, might serve Him without fear, in holiness and righteousness before Him all the days of our lives.

—LUKE 1:74–75

So he said to the vinedresser of his vineyard, "Now these three years I have come looking for fruit on this fig tree, and I find none. Cut it down. Why should it deplete the soil?"

—LUKE 13:7

## John

A new commandment I give to you, that you love one another, even as I have loved you, that you also love one another. By this all men will know that you are My disciples, if you have love for one another.

—JOHN 13:34–35

Every branch in Me that bears no fruit, He takes away. And every branch that bears fruit, He prunes, that it may bear more fruit.

—John 15:2

Sanctify them by Your truth. Your word is truth.

—John 17:17

For their sakes I sanctify Myself, that they also may be sanctified by the truth.

—John 17:19

## Acts

But that we write to them to abstain from food offered to idols, from sexual immorality, from strangled animals, and from blood.

—Acts 15:20

Abstain from food offered to idols, from sexual immorality, from strangled animals, and from blood. If you keep yourselves from these, you will do well. Farewell.

—Acts 15:29

As for the Gentiles who believe, we have written and concluded that they should observe no such thing, except that they abstain from food offered to idols, from sexual immorality, from strangled animals, and from blood.

—Acts 21:25

## Romans

And declared to be the Son of God with power, according to the Spirit of holiness, by the resurrection from the dead.

—ROMANS 1:4

To all who are in Rome, beloved of God, called to be saints: Grace to you and peace from God our Father and the Lord Jesus Christ.

—ROMANS 1:7

You who boast in the law, do you dishonor God through breaking the law? As it is written, "The name of God is blasphemed among the Gentiles because of you."

—ROMANS 2:23–24

Being justified freely by His grace through the redemption that is in Christ Jesus.

—ROMANS 3:24

Therefore we conclude that a man is justified by faith without the works of the law.

—ROMANS 3:28

Knowing this, that our old man has been crucified with Him, so that the body of sin might be destroyed, and we should no longer be slaves to sin.

—ROMANS 6:6

I speak in human terms because of the weakness of your flesh, for just as you have yielded your members as slaves to impurity and iniquity leading to more iniquity, even so now yield your members as slaves to righteousness unto holiness.

—ROMANS 6:19

But now, having been freed from sin and having become slaves of God, you have fruit unto holiness, and the end is eternal life.

—ROMANS 6:22

To be carnally minded is death, but to be spiritually minded is life and peace, for the carnal mind is hostile toward God, for it is not subject to the law of God, nor indeed can it be.

—ROMANS 8:6–7

For if you live according to the flesh, you will die, but if through the Spirit you put to death the deeds of the body, you will live.

—ROMANS 8:13

I urge you therefore, brothers, by the mercies of God, that you present your bodies as a living sacrifice, holy, and acceptable to God, which is your reasonable service of worship. Do not be conformed to this world, but be transformed by the renewing of your mind, that you may prove what is the good and acceptable and perfect will of God.

—ROMANS 12:1–2

# 1 Corinthians

To the church of God which is at Corinth, to those who are sanctified in Christ Jesus, called to be saints, with all who in every place call on the name of Jesus Christ our Lord, both their Lord and ours.

—1 CORINTHIANS 1:2

These things also we proclaim, not in the words which man's wisdom teaches, but which the Holy Spirit teaches, comparing spiritual things with spiritual.

—1 CORINTHIANS 2:13

If anyone defiles the temple of God, God will destroy him. For the temple of God is holy. And you are His temple.

—1 CORINTHIANS 3:17

Therefore purge out the old yeast, that you may be a new batch, since you are unleavened. For even Christ, our Passover, has been sacrificed for us.

—1 CORINTHIANS 5:7

Do you not know that the saints will judge the world? If the world will be judged by you, are you unworthy to judge the smallest matters?

—1 CORINTHIANS 6:2

Do you not know that the unrighteous will not inherit the kingdom of God? Do not be deceived. Neither the sexually immoral, nor idolaters, nor adulterers, nor male prostitutes, nor homosexuals, nor thieves, nor covetous, nor drunkards, nor revilers, nor extortioners will inherit the kingdom of God. Such were some of you. But you were washed, you were sanctified, and you were justified in the name of the Lord Jesus by the Spirit of our God.

—1 CORINTHIANS 6:9–11

If I speak with the tongues of men and of angels, and have not love, I have become as sounding brass or a clanging cymbal. If I have the gift of prophecy, and understand all mysteries and all knowledge, and if I have all faith, so that I could remove mountains, and have not love, I am nothing. If I give all my goods to feed the poor, and if I give my body to be burned, and have not love, it profits me nothing.

—1 CORINTHIANS 13:1–3

One who speaks in a tongue edifies himself; but one who prophesies edifies the church [promotes growth in spiritual wisdom, devotion, holiness, and joy].

—1 CORINTHIANS 14:4, AMP

## 2 Corinthians

What agreement has Christ with Belial? Or what part has he who believes with an unbeliever? What agreement has the temple of God with idols? For you are the temple of the living God. As God has said:

"I will live in them
and walk in them.
I will be their God,
and they shall be My people."
Therefore,
"Come out from among them
and be separate,
says the Lord.
Do not touch what is unclean,
and I will receive you."
"I will be a Father to you,
and you shall be My sons and daughters,
says the Lord Almighty."

—2 Corinthians 6:15–18

Since we have these promises, beloved, let us cleanse ourselves from all filthiness of the flesh and spirit, perfecting holiness in the fear of God.

—2 Corinthians 7:1

## Galatians

Yet we know that a man is not justified by the works of the law, but through faith in Jesus Christ. Even we have believed in Christ Jesus, so that we might be justified by faith in Christ, rather than by the works of the law. For by the works of the law no flesh shall be justified.

—Galatians 2:16

I have been crucified with Christ. It is no longer I who live, but Christ who lives in me. And the life I now live in the flesh, I live by faith in the Son of God, who loved me and gave Himself for me.

—GALATIANS 2:20

O foolish Galatians! Who has bewitched you that you should not obey the truth? Before your eyes Jesus Christ was clearly portrayed among you as crucified.

—GALATIANS 3:1

You, brothers, have been called to liberty. Only do not use liberty to give an opportunity to the flesh, but by love serve one another.

—GALATIANS 5:13

I say then, walk in the Spirit, and you shall not fulfill the lust of the flesh.

—GALATIANS 5:16

Those who are Christ's have crucified the flesh with its passions and lusts. If we live in the Spirit, let us also walk in the Spirit.

—GALATIANS 5:24–25

Be not deceived. God is not mocked. For whatever a man sows, that will he also reap. For the one who sows to his own flesh will from the flesh reap corruption, but the one who sows to the Spirit will from the Spirit reap eternal life.

—GALATIANS 6:7–8

God forbid that I should boast, except in the cross of our Lord Jesus Christ, by whom the world is crucified to me, and I to the world.

—Galatians 6:14

## Ephesians

Just as He chose us in Him before the foundation of the world, to be holy and blameless before Him in love.

—Ephesians 1:4

Now, therefore, you are no longer strangers and foreigners, but are fellow citizens with the saints and members of the household of God.

—Ephesians 2:19

And that you put on the new nature, which was created according to God in righteousness and true holiness.

—Ephesians 4:24

Let no unwholesome word proceed out of your mouth, but only that which is good for building up, that it may give grace to the listeners.

—Ephesians 4:29

And do not let sexual immorality, or any impurity, or greed be named among you, as these are not proper among saints. Let there be no filthiness, nor foolish talking, nor coarse joking, which are not fitting. Instead, give thanks.

—Ephesians 5:3–4

That He might sanctify and cleanse it with the washing of water by the word, and that He might present to Himself a glorious church, not having spot, or wrinkle, or any such thing, but that it should be holy and without blemish.

—EPHESIANS 5:26–27

## Colossians

To the saints and faithful brothers in Christ who are at Colosse: Grace to you and peace from God our Father and the Lord Jesus Christ.

—COLOSSIANS 1:2

In the body of His flesh through death, to present you holy and blameless and above reproach in His sight.

—COLOSSIANS 1:22

Therefore put to death the parts of your earthly nature: sexual immorality, uncleanness, inordinate affection, evil desire, and covetousness, which is idolatry.

—COLOSSIANS 3:5

But now you must also put away all these: anger, wrath, malice, blasphemy, and filthy language out of your mouth.

—COLOSSIANS 3:8

So embrace, as the elect of God, holy and beloved, a spirit of mercy, kindness, humbleness of mind, meekness, and longsuffering.

—Colossians 3:12

# 1 Thessalonians

To this end may He establish your hearts to be blameless in holiness before our God and Father at the coming of our Lord Jesus Christ with all His saints.

—1 Thessalonians 3:13

For you know what commands we gave you through the Lord Jesus. For this is the will of God, your sanctification: that you should abstain from sexual immorality, that each one of you should know how to possess his own vessel in sanctification and honor.

—1 Thessalonians 4:2–4

For God has not called us to uncleanness, but to holiness.

—1 Thessalonians 4:7

May the very God of peace sanctify you completely. And I pray to God that your whole spirit, soul, and body be preserved blameless unto the coming of our Lord Jesus Christ.

—1 Thessalonians 5:23

# 1 Timothy

Therefore I desire that the men pray everywhere, lifting up holy hands, without wrath or contentiousness.

—1 TIMOTHY 2:8

For bodily exercise profits a little, but godliness is profitable in all things, holding promise for the present life and also for the life to come.

—1 TIMOTHY 4:8

But godliness with contentment is great gain.

—1 TIMOTHY 6:6

But you, O man of God, escape these things, and follow after righteousness, godliness, faith, love, patience, and gentleness.

—1 TIMOTHY 6:11

# 2 Timothy

Who has saved us and called us with a holy calling, not by our works, but by His own purpose and grace, which was given us in Christ Jesus before the world began.

—2 TIMOTHY 1:9

But the firm foundation of God stands, having this seal, "The Lord knows those who are His," and, "Let everyone who calls on the name of Christ depart from iniquity."

In a large house there are not only gold and

silver vessels, but also those of wood and clay; some are for honor, and some for dishonor. One who cleanses himself from these things will be a vessel for honor, sanctified, fit for the Master's use, and prepared for every good work.

—2 TIMOTHY 2:19–21

Having a form of godliness, but denying its power. Turn away from such people.

—2 TIMOTHY 3:5

Yes, and all who desire to live a godly life in Christ Jesus will suffer persecution.

—2 TIMOTHY 3:12

## Titus

For an overseer must be blameless, as a steward of God, not self-willed, not easily angered, not given to drunkenness, not violent, not greedy for dishonest gain, but hospitable, a lover of what is good, self-controlled, just, holy, temperate.

—TITUS 1:7–8

Likewise, older women should be reverent in behavior, and not be false accusers, not be enslaved to much wine, but teachers of good things.

—TITUS 2:3

For the grace of God that brings salvation has appeared to all men, teaching us that, denying ungodliness and worldly desires, we should live soberly, righteously, and in godliness in this present world.

—TITUS 2:11–12

Who gave Himself for us, that He might redeem us from all lawlessness and purify for Himself a special people, zealous of good works.

—TITUS 2:14

## Hebrews

For such a High Priest was fitting for us, for He is holy, innocent, undefiled, separate from sinners, and is higher than the heavens.

—HEBREWS 7:26

How much more shall the blood of Christ, who through the eternal Spirit offered Himself without blemish to God, cleanse your conscience from dead works to serve the living God?

—HEBREWS 9:14

Let us draw near with a true heart in full assurance of faith, having our hearts sprinkled to cleanse them from an evil conscience, and our bodies washed with pure water.

—HEBREWS 10:22

For they indeed disciplined us for a short time according to their own judgment, but He does so for our profit, that we may partake of His holiness.

—HEBREWS 12:10

Pursue peace with all men, and the holiness without which no one will see the Lord, watching diligently so that no one falls short of the grace of God, lest any root of bitterness spring up to cause trouble, and many become defiled by it.

—Hebrews 12:14–15

Therefore, since we are receiving a kingdom that cannot be moved, let us be gracious, by which we may serve God acceptably with reverence and godly fear.

—Hebrews 12:28

Marriage is to be honored among everyone, and the bed undefiled. But God will judge the sexually immoral and adulterers.

—Hebrews 13:4

## James

Religion that is pure and undefiled before God, the Father, is this: to visit the fatherless and widows in their affliction and to keep oneself unstained by the world.

—James 1:27

Was not Abraham our father justified by works when he offered his son Isaac on the altar?

—James 2:21

You see then how by works a man is justified, and not by faith only. Likewise, was not Rahab the prostitute justified by works when she received the messengers and sent them out another way?

—James 2:24–25

The tongue is a fire, a world of evil. The tongue is among the parts of the body, defiling the whole body, and setting the course of nature on fire, and it is set on fire by hell.

—James 3:6

But the wisdom that is from above is first pure, then peaceable, gentle, open to reason, full of mercy and good fruits, without partiality, and without hypocrisy.

—James 3:17

Draw near to God, and He will draw near to you. Cleanse your hands, you sinners, and purify your hearts, you double-minded.

—James 4:8

## 1 Peter

But as He who has called you is holy, so be holy in all your conduct, because it is written, "Be holy, for I am holy."

—1 Peter 1:15–16

Since your souls have been purified by obedience to the truth through the Spirit unto a genuine brotherly love, love one another deeply with a pure heart.

—1 Peter 1:22

You also, as living stones, are being built up into a spiritual house as a holy priesthood to offer up spiritual sacrifices that are acceptable to God through Jesus Christ.

—1 Peter 2:5

But you are a chosen race, a royal priesthood, a holy nation, a people for God's own possession, so that you may declare the goodness of Him who has called you out of darkness into His marvelous light.

—1 Peter 2:9

## 2 Peter

His divine power has given to us all things that pertain to life and godliness through the knowledge of Him who has called us by His own glory and excellence.

—2 Peter 1:3

For it would have been better for them not to have known the way of righteousness than to have known it and then turn back from the holy commandment that was delivered to them. But it has happened to them according to the true proverb, "The dog returns to his own vomit," and "the sow that was washed to her wallowing in the mud."

—2 Peter 2:21–22

## 1 John

But if we walk in the light as He is in the light, we have fellowship one with another, and the blood of Jesus Christ His Son cleanses us from all sin.

—1 John 1:7

If we confess our sins, He is faithful and just to forgive us our sins and cleanse us from all unrighteousness.

—1 John 1:9

Do not love the world or the things in the world. If anyone loves the world, the love of the Father is not in him. For all that is in the world—the lust of the flesh, the lust of the eyes, and the pride of life—is not of the Father, but is of the world.

—1 John 2:15–16

## Revelation

But I have a few things against you: You have there those who hold the teaching of Balaam, who taught Balak to cast a stumbling block before the children of Israel, to eat things sacrificed to idols and to commit sexual immorality.

—Revelation 2:14

But I have a few things against you: You permit that woman Jezebel, who calls herself a prophetess, to teach and seduce My servants to commit sexual immorality and eat food sacrificed to idols. I gave her time to repent of her sexual immorality, but she did not repent.

—Revelation 2:20–21

The four living creatures had six wings each, and they were covered with eyes all around. All day and night, without ceasing, they were saying: "'Holy, holy, holy, Lord God Almighty,' who was, and is, and is to come."

—Revelation 4:8

Here is the patience of the saints; here are those who keep the commandments of God and the faith of Jesus.

—Revelation 14:12

They sang the song of Moses, the servant of God, and the song of the Lamb, saying:

"Great and marvelous are Your works,
 Lord God Almighty!
Just and true are Your ways,
 O King of saints!
Who shall not fear You, O Lord,
 and glorify Your name?
For You alone are holy.
All nations shall come
 and worship before You,
 for Your judgments have been revealed."

—Revelation 15:3–4

"It was granted her to be arrayed in fine linen, clean and white." Fine linen is the righteous deeds of the saints.

—REVELATION 19:8

The armies in heaven, clothed in fine linen, white and clean, followed Him on white horses.

—REVELATION 19:14

I, John, saw the Holy City, the New Jerusalem, coming down out of heaven from God, prepared as a bride adorned for her husband.

—REVELATION 21:2

And he carried me away in the Spirit to a great and high mountain, and showed me the Holy City, Jerusalem, descending out of heaven from God.

—REVELATION 21:10

# PART III

# SCRIPTURES ON THE **NATURE OF GOD**

# 7

# THERE IS NONE LIKE YOU

Exodus 3:13–14 says, "Moses said to God, 'I am going to the children of Israel and will say to them, "The God of your fathers has sent me to you." When they say to me, "What is His name?" what shall I say to them?' And God said to Moses, 'I AM WHO I AM,' and He said, 'You will say this to the children of Israel, "I AM has sent me to you."'"

God *is* His name. Yes, God's name is His character. He is known by many names throughout the Bible that reflect His character, attributes, and ways. Understanding the names of God will help you understand His nature—who He is. Here's a list of the common names of God used in the Bible:[1]

- *Adonai* (Lord, Master)—In the Old Testament *Adonai* occurs 434 times. There are heavy uses of *Adonai* in Isaiah as "Adonai Jehovah." It occurs two hundred times in Ezekiel alone and appears eleven times in Daniel chapter 9. *Adonai* is first used in Genesis 15:2.

- *El Shaddai* means "Lord God Almighty." This name speaks of God's power and mighty acts. In the Old Testament El Shaddai occurs seven times. El Shaddai is first used in Genesis 17:1.

- *Elohim* means "God"—In the Old Testament *Elohim* occurs over two thousand times. *Elohim* is first used in Genesis 1:1.

- *I am that I am* was revealed to Moses. This name of God provides an unlimited number of words that can reveal God's nature: shield, deliverer, healer, provider, friend, and so on. When Moses saw the burning bush in the desert, he asked God, "When they say to me, 'What is His name?' what shall I say to them?" God answered his question by the revelation of His name as the "I Am." "And God said to Moses, 'I AM WHO I AM,' and He said, 'You will say this to the children of Israel, "I AM has sent me to you"'" (Exod. 3:13–14).

- *Jehovah Jireh* (the Lord Will Provide)—The name given by Abraham at the place where he almost slayed his son Isaac (Gen. 22:14).

- *Jehovah M'Kaddesh* means "the Lord Who Sanctifies You." A God separate from all that is evil requires that the people who follow Him be cleansed from all evil. When He says, "Be holy as I am holy," He provides a way for us to be more like Him through the process of sanctification ("I am the LORD who sanctifies you" [Exod. 31:13]). This aspect of God was revealed in part 2 of this book.

- *Jehovah Nissi* means "the Lord My Banner." This speaks of the God of victory and triumph. (See Exodus 17:15.)

- *Jehovah Rapha* (the Lord Who Heals)— When God brought the people of Israel to Marah, He became known as "the Lord who heals you" (Exod. 15:26). This is the place where He turned bitter water sweet— He healed the waters.

- *Jehovah Rohi* (sometimes *Jehovah Raah*) means "the Lord My Shepherd." This name speaks of the Lord's protection, leading, feeding, and the like. The most extensive reference to this aspect of God's character is Psalm 23.

- *Jehovah Sabaoth* means "the Lord of Hosts"—It appears many times throughout the Bible (1 Sam. 1:11; 17:45; 2 Sam. 6:18; 7:27; 1 Kings 19:14; 2 Kings 3:14; 1 Chron. 11:9; Ps. 24:10; 48:8; 80:4, 19; 84:3; Isa. 1:24; 3:15; 5:16; 6:5; 9:19; 10:26; 14:22; Jer. 9:15; 48:1; Hosea 12:5; Amos 3:13; Micah 4:4; Nah. 3:5; Hag. 2:6; Zech. 1:3; Mal. 1:6; Hab. 2:13; Zeph. 2:9).

- *Jehovah Shalom* means the "Lord Is Peace." The peace of God, or shalom, includes prosperity, health, and wholeness. Gideon named the place where God confirmed his victory over the Midianites "the Lord Is Peace," and he built an altar (Judg. 6:24).

- *Jehovah Shammah* means "the Lord Is There" (or the Lord Is Present). Jehovah Shammah is a Christian transliteration of the Hebrew, meaning "Jehovah is there," the name given to the city in Ezekiel's vision in Ezekiel 48:35.

- *Wonderful*—God is a God of wonders. This name speaks of the wonderful works of God. *Wonderful* means "inspiring delight, pleasure, or admiration; extremely good; marvellous."[2]

## God Is Where His Presence Dwells

Another important aspect of who God is, is His presence or His glory. Knowing His character will cause us to want to be in His presence. Glory is a manifestation of God's presence. Shekinah glory is a visible manifestation of His presence. Glory is a major theme in the Scriptures. God is a God of glory (Ps. 29:3) and the King of glory (Ps. 24:10). The Father is the Father of glory (Eph. 1:7). The Son is the Lord of glory (1 Cor. 2:8; James 2:1). The Holy Spirit is the Spirit of glory (1 Pet. 4:14).

Glory produces wealth, riches, honor, and prosperity. Glory brings salvation, healing, and restoration. Glory attracts. Glory promotes. Glory transforms. Glory releases miracles. Glory protects, covers, and shields.

## The Cloud of Glory

As believers, we should desire to live under a cloud of glory. There are many benefits to being in the cloud of God's glory.

The cloud is a symbol of God's covering and protection.

> I would not want you to be unaware that all our fathers were under the cloud, and all passed through the sea.
> —1 CORINTHIANS 10:1

Also, Isaiah 4:5 says, "For upon all the glory shall be a defence" (KJV). Again, the cloud is for protection and defense. Those who live under the cloud live under God's protection and defense.

The Lord will appear to us in the cloud of glory:

> So as Aaron spoke to the whole congregation of the children of Israel, they looked toward the wilderness, and indeed, the glory of the LORD appeared in the cloud.
>
> —Exodus 16:10

The Lord will descend upon us and stand with us in the cloud of glory:

> Then the LORD descended in the cloud, and stood with him there, and proclaimed the name of the LORD.
>
> —Exodus 34:5

God speaks to us in the cloud:

> He spoke to them in the pillar of cloud; they kept His statues and the ordinance that He gave them.
>
> —Psalm 99:7

Strong prophetic utterances come to us in the cloud. The Lord will speak to churches that are under the cloud:

> By His knowledge the depths are broken up, and the clouds drop down the dew.
>
> —Proverbs 3:20

God has promised to put His cloud over Zion:

> Then the LORD will create upon every dwelling place
> of Mount Zion, and upon her assemblies, a cloud
> and smoke by day and the shining of a flaming fire
> by night. For over all the glory shall be a covering.
> —ISAIAH 4:5

When we live under the cloud, the glory of the Lord will fill our houses and our churches. So not only should individual believers seek to live under the cloud, but also churches should live under the cloud.

Don't ever let the cloud depart. Seek to remain under the cloud and live under the glory of God.

## Radiating the Glory of God

God's glory radiates from our countenance. Psalm 34:5 says, "They looked to Him and became radiant, and their faces are not ashamed." You can have a radiant countenance, one that reflects the glory of God. Your countenance is important. You can also have a sad countenance or a cheerful countenance. Your cheerful countenance reflects the glory of God. Countenance has to do with your appearance, facial expressions, and body language. Your countenance is a reflection of your heart. If you have been in the presence of God and covered by His glory, your countenance should beam with joy.

The word *radiant* means "sending out rays of light; bright; shining; characterized by health, intense joy."[3]

Stephen in the Bible is an example of someone who had a radiant countenance.

> All who sat in the Sanhedrin, gazing at [Stephen], saw his face as the face of an angel.
> —ACTS 6:15

There was a time when a small group of believers and I were crossing the border from Mozambique to South Africa. We told the border patrol agent that we were Christians, and he said, "I know. I can tell by your faces."

Moses is another example of a person who had a radiant countenance. Being in the presence of God will affect your countenance:

> When Moses came down from Mount Sinai with the two tablets of testimony in the hands of Moses, when he came down from the mountain, Moses did not know that the skin of his face shone while he talked with Him. So when Aaron and all the children of Israel saw Moses, amazingly, the skin of his face shone, and they were afraid to come near him.
> —EXODUS 34:29–30

According to Psalm 42:11, God is the health of your countenance. A radiant countenance is a healthy countenance: "Why art thou cast down, O my soul? and why art thou disquieted within me? hope thou in God: for I shall yet praise him, who is the health of my countenance, and my God" (KJV).

As believers, we should be radiant with the glory of God. We should radiate His brightness and light.

It was always the plan of God for the earth to be filled with His glory and for the people of God to dwell in His glory. His church is a glorious church. A revelation of the glory of God will help you live and operate in the glory realm. There are certain blessings that are connected to the glory, and we should develop a knowledge of the glory of the Lord so we can partake in these blessings.

Meditating and praying the Scriptures and promises related to God's glory, character, and ways builds faith, courage, and boldness in our hearts. It increases the presence of God in our lives and sets us on a path of fruitfulness and success.

The glory realm—the realm of God's manifest presence—is the place where the supernatural dwells. Miracles take place in God's presence and glory. Change and transformation take place in the glory and presence of God. The Bible says that by beholding the glory of the Lord, we become changed.

> But we all, seeing the glory of the Lord with unveiled faces, as in a mirror, are being transformed into the same image from glory to glory by the Spirit of the Lord.
>
> —2 Corinthians 3:18

If you want to walk in miracles and the supernatural, if you want to see signs and wonders, stay in the glory.

Let's take a look now at how the ways of God and His glory are displayed in His Word. Again, included are verses that address God's character and glory, as well as scriptures that show manifestations of the opposite of what we want to see in our lives.

# 8

# GOD IN THE OLD TESTAMENT

In the Old Testament God's glory is represented by several Hebrew words. One is *kabowd*, which means "weight," "abundance," "honor," "glory," "splendor," "wealth," "riches," "reverence," "dignity."[1] It also means "reputation."[2] God's glory is His reputation. *Kabowd* is used about two hundred times in the Old Testament.

Another word is *shekinah*, which is the visible majesty of the divine presence of God, especially when resting or dwelling between the cherubim on the mercy seat, in the tabernacle. (See Exodus 25:22; Leviticus 16:2; 2 Samuel 6:2; 2 Kings 19:14–15; Psalm 80:1; Isaiah 37:16; Ezekiel 9:3; 10:18; Hebrews 9:5.)[3]

Another word for glory in the Old Testament is *no'am*, translated as "beauty" (Ps. 27:4), "pleasant," and "pleasantness," and means "splendor or grace."[4]

The key verses for this chapter are Habakkuk 2:14: "For the earth shall be filled with the knowledge of the glory of the LORD, as the waters cover the sea" (KJV); and

2 Chronicles 5:14, "So that the priests could not stand to minister by reason of the cloud: for the glory of the Lord had filled the house of God." (kjv).

## Genesis

Then they heard the sound of the Lord God walking in the garden in the cool of the day, and the man and his wife hid themselves from the presence of the Lord God among the trees of the garden.

—Genesis 3:8

## Exodus

Your right hand, O Lord, is glorious in power. Your right hand, O Lord, shatters the enemy.

—Exodus 15:6

Who is like You, O Lord, among the gods? Who is like You, glorious in holiness, fearful in praises, doing wonders?

—Exodus 15:11

Who is like You among the gods, O Lord? Who is like You, majestic in holiness, awesome in splendor, working wonders?

—Exodus 15:11, amp

Miriam answered them, "Sing to the Lord, for He triumphed gloriously! The horse and his rider He has hurled into the sea."

—Exodus 15:21

And in the morning you shall see the glory of the LORD, because He hears your murmurings against the LORD. And what are we that you murmur against us?

—EXODUS 16:7

So as Aaron spoke to the whole congregation of the children of Israel, they looked toward the wilderness, and indeed, the glory of the LORD appeared in the cloud.

—EXODUS 16:10

So on the third day, in the morning, there was thunder and lightning, and a thick cloud on the mountain, and the sound of an exceedingly loud trumpet. All the people who were in the camp trembled.

—EXODUS 19:16

All the people witnessed the thunder and the lightning and the sound of the trumpet and the mountain smoking; and when the people saw it, they trembled and stood at a distance.

—EXODUS 20:18

The glory of the LORD rested on Mount Sinai, and the cloud covered it for six days. And on the seventh day He called to Moses from the midst of the cloud.

—EXODUS 24:16

In the sight of the Israelites the appearance of the glory and brilliance of the LORD was like consuming fire on the top of the mountain.

—Exodus 24:17, AMP

Now the appearance of the glory of the LORD was like a consuming fire on the top of the mountain to the eyes of the children of Israel.

—Exodus 24:17

I will meet with you there, and I will meet with you from above the mercy seat, from between the two cherubim which are upon the ark of the testimony. I will speak with you all that I will command you for the children of Israel.

—Exodus 25:22

I will meet there with the children of Israel, and it will be consecrated by My glory.

—Exodus 29:43

And He said, "My Presence will go with you, and I will give you rest." Then he said to Him, "If Your Presence does not go with us, do not bring us up from here."

—Exodus 33:14–15

Then Moses said, "I pray, show me Your glory."

—Exodus 33:18

While My glory passes by, I will put you in a cleft of the rock and will cover you with My hand while I pass by.

—Exodus 33:22

When Moses came down from Mount Sinai with the two tablets of testimony in the hands of Moses, when he came down from the mountain, Moses did not know that the skin of his face shone while he talked with Him. So when Aaron and all the children of Israel saw Moses, amazingly, the skin of his face shone, and they were afraid to come near him.

—Exodus 34:29–30

When Moses finished speaking with them, he put a veil over his face.

—Exodus 34:33

The children of Israel saw the face of Moses, that the skin of Moses' face shone, and then Moses put the veil over his face again until he went in to speak with Him.

—Exodus 34:35

Then the cloud covered the tent of meeting, and the glory of the LORD filled the tabernacle.

—Exodus 40:34

Then the cloud [the Shekinah, God's visible, dwelling presence] covered the Tent of Meeting, and the glory and brilliance of the LORD filled the tabernacle.

—Exodus 40:34, AMP

Moses was not able to enter into the tent of meeting because the cloud settled on it, and the glory of the Lord filled the tabernacle.

—Exodus 40:35

## Leviticus

Moses said, "This is the thing which the Lord commanded that you should do; then the glory of the Lord shall appear to you."

—Leviticus 9:6

Moses and Aaron went into the tent of meeting, and when they came out they blessed the people, and the glory of the Lord appeared to all the people.

—Leviticus 9:23

## Numbers

But all the assembly said, "Stone them with stones." And the glory of the Lord appeared at the tent of meeting before all the children of Israel.

—Numbers 14:10

But truly as I live, all the earth will be filled with the glory of the Lord.

—Numbers 14:21

Because all those men seeing My glory and My signs which I did in Egypt and in the wilderness, and have tempted Me now these ten times, and have not listened to My voice.

—Numbers 14:22

Korah gathered all the assembly against them to the door of the tent of meeting, and the glory of the LORD appeared to all the assembly.

—NUMBERS 16:19

When the assembly was gathered against Moses and Aaron, they looked toward the tent of meeting. The cloud covered it, and the glory of the LORD appeared.

—NUMBERS 16:42

Moses and Aaron went from the presence of the assembly to the door of the tent of meeting, and they fell on their faces, and the glory of the LORD appeared to them.

—NUMBERS 20:6

## Deuteronomy

You said, "See, the LORD our God has shown us His glory and His greatness, and we have heard His voice from the midst of the fire. We have seen this day that God speaks with man, yet he lives."

—DEUTERONOMY 5:24

If you are not careful to observe all the words of this law that are written in this book so that you may fear this glorious and fearful name, the LORD your God, then the LORD will bring extraordinary plagues on you and your descendants, even great long-lasting plagues, and severe and long-lasting sicknesses.

—Deuteronomy 28:58

He said: The Lord came from Sinai and rose up from Seir to them; He shone forth from Mount Paran, and He came with ten thousands of holy ones; from His right hand went a fiery law for them.

—Deuteronomy 33:2

His glory is like the firstborn of his bull, and his horns are like the horns of a wild ox; with them he will push the peoples together to the ends of the earth; they are the ten thousands of Ephraim, and they are the thousands of Manasseh.

—Deuteronomy 33:17

# 1 Samuel

He raises up the poor out of the dust and lifts up the oppressed from the dunghill to make them sit with princes and inherit a throne of glory. "For the pillars of the earth belong to the Lord, and He has set the world upon them."

—1 Samuel 2:8

She named the child Ichabod, saying, "The glory is departed from Israel," because the ark of God was taken, and because of her father-in-law and her husband.

—1 Samuel 4:21

She said, "The glory is departed from Israel, for the ark of God is taken."

—1 Samuel 4:22

## 2 Samuel

From the brightness before Him embers of fire are kindled. The Lord thundered from heaven, and the Most High uttered His voice.

—2 Samuel 22:13–14

## 1 Kings

So that the priests could not continue to minister because of the cloud, for the glory of the Lord filled the house of the Lord.

—1 Kings 8:11

Now the weight of the gold that came to Solomon in one [particular] year was six hundred and sixty-six talents of gold.

—1 Kings 10:14, amp

## 1 Chronicles

Glory in His holy name; let the heart of those who seek the Lord rejoice.

—1 Chronicles 16:10

Declare His glory among the nations, His wonders among all the peoples.

—1 Chronicles 16:24

Honor and majesty are before Him; strength and joy are in His place.

—1 Chronicles 16:27

Give to the Lord, O families of the peoples, give to the Lord glory and strength.

—1 Chronicles 16:28

Give to the Lord the glory due His name; bring an offering and come before Him, bow down to the Lord in holy array.

—1 Chronicles 16:29

Now say, "Save us, O God of our salvation, and gather us and deliver us from the nations, that we may give thanks to Your holy name, to glory in Your praise."

—1 Chronicles 16:35

Now David said, "Solomon my son is young and inexperienced, and the house that is to be built for the Lord must be exceedingly magnificent, of fame and glory throughout all the lands. Therefore I will make preparation for it now." So David made extensive preparations before his death.

—1 Chronicles 22:5

Yours, O Lord, is the greatness, and the power, and the glory, and the victory, and the majesty, for everything in the heavens and the earth is Yours. Yours is the kingdom, O Lord, and You exalt Yourself as head above all.

—1 Chronicles 29:11

So now, our God, we give thanks to You, and praise Your glorious name.

—1 CHRONICLES 29:13

The LORD highly exalted Solomon in the sight of all Israel and bestowed on him such royal majesty as had never been on any king in Israel before him.

—1 CHRONICLES 29:25

## 2 Chronicles

And the priests were not able to stand in order to serve because of the cloud, for the glory of the LORD had filled the house of God.

—2 CHRONICLES 5:14

And when Solomon finished praying, fire came down from the heavens and consumed the burnt offering and sacrifices, and the glory of the LORD filled the temple.

—2 CHRONICLES 7:1

And the priests were not able to enter into the house of the LORD, for the glory of the LORD filled the LORD's house.

—2 CHRONICLES 7:2

And all the sons of Israel saw when the fire came down and the glory of the LORD came on the temple, and they bowed their faces low to the ground on the pavement, and they worshipped confessing, "The Lord is good, and His mercy endures forever."

—2 Chronicles 7:3

## Nehemiah

Then the Levites, Jeshua, Kadmiel, Bani, Hashabneiah, Sherebiah, Hodiah, Shebaniah, and Pethahiah, said: "Stand up and bless the Lord your God forever and ever! Let them bless Your glorious name, which is exalted above all blessing and praise."

—Nehemiah 9:5

## Esther

He unveiled the riches of his glorious kingdom and the costly luxury of his greatness for many days, one hundred and eighty days.

—Esther 1:4

## Job

He has stripped me of my glory and taken the crown from my head.

—Job 19:9

My glory was fresh in me, and my bow was renewed in my hand.

—Job 29:20

God thunders marvelously with His voice; He does great things that we cannot comprehend.

—Job 37:5

Have you an arm like God? Or can you thunder with a voice like Him? Adorn yourself now with majesty and excellence, and array yourself with glory and beauty.

—Job 40:9–10

## Psalms

But You, O Lord, are a shield for me, my glory and the One who raises up my head.

—Psalm 3:3

O people, how long will you turn my glory into shame? How long will you love vanity and seek after lies? Selah.

—Psalm 4:2

O Lord, our Lord, how excellent is Your name in all the earth! You have set Your glory above the heavens.

—Psalm 8:1

For You have made him a little lower than the angels, and crowned him with glory and honor.

—Psalm 8:5

When my enemies are turned back, they will stumble and perish at Your presence.

—Psalm 9:3

Therefore my heart is glad, and my glory rejoices; my flesh also will rest in security.

—PSALM 16:9

You will make known to me the path of life; in Your presence is fullness of joy; at Your right hand there are pleasures for evermore.

—PSALM 16:11

At the brightness before Him His thick clouds passed by, hailstones and coals of fire.

—PSALM 18:12

The heavens declare the glory of God, and the firmament shows His handiwork. Day unto day utters speech, and night unto night declares knowledge. There is no speech and there are no words; their voice is not heard.

—PSALM 19:1–3

His glory is great in Your salvation; honor and majesty You set on him.

—PSALM 21:5

Lift up your heads, O you gates; and be lifted up, you everlasting doors, that the King of glory may enter.

—PSALM 24:7

Who is this King of glory? The LORD strong and mighty, the LORD mighty in battle.

—PSALM 24:8

Lift up your heads, O you gates; lift up, you ever-lasting doors, that the King of glory may enter.

—Psalm 24:9

Who is He—this King of glory? The Lord of Hosts, He is the King of glory. Selah.

—Psalm 24:10

One thing I have asked from the Lord, that will I seek after—for me to dwell in the house of the Lord all the days of my life, to see the beauty of the Lord, and to inquire in His temple.

—Psalm 27:4

One thing I have asked of the Lord, and that I will seek: That I may dwell in the house of the Lord [in His presence] all the days of my life, to gaze upon the beauty [the delightful loveliness and majestic grandeur] of the Lord and to meditate in His temple.

—Psalm 27:4, amp

Give to the Lord, you heavenly beings, give to the Lord glory and strength.

—Psalm 29:1

Give to the Lord the glory of His name; worship the Lord in holy splendor.

—Psalm 29:2

The voice of the Lord is over the waters; the God of glory thunders; the Lord is over many waters.

—Psalm 29:3

The voice of the Lord sounds with strength; the voice of the Lord—with majesty.

—Psalm 29:4

The voice of the Lord makes the deer to give birth, and strips the forests bare; and in His temple everyone says, "Glory!"

—Psalm 29:9

So that my glory may sing praise to You and not be silent. O Lord my God, I will give thanks to You forever.

—Psalm 30:12

You will hide them in the secret of Your presence from conspirators; You will keep them secretly in a shelter from the strife of tongues.

—Psalm 31:20

They looked to Him and were radiant; their faces will never blush in shame or confusion.

—Psalm 34:5, amp

Gird your sword on your thigh, O mighty one, with your splendor and your majesty. In your majesty ride prosperously because of truth and meekness and righteousness; and your right hand will teach you awesome things.

—Psalm 45:3–4

The royal daughter is all glorious within her chamber; her clothing is plaited gold.

—Psalm 45:13

Do not fear when one is made rich, when the glory of his house is increased.

—Psalm 49:16

For he takes nothing away in death; his glory does not descend after him.

—Psalm 49:17

Out of Zion, the perfection of beauty, God has shined.

—Psalm 50:2

Be exalted, O God, above the heavens; may Your glory be above all the earth.

—Psalm 57:5

Awake, my glory! Awake, psaltery and harp! I will awake the dawn.

—Psalm 57:8

Be exalted, O God, above the heavens; may Your glory be above all the earth.

—Psalm 57:11

In God is my salvation and my glory; the rock of my strength, and my shelter, is in God.

—Psalm 62:7

I have seen You in the sanctuary, to see Your power and Your glory.

—Psalm 63:2

But the king will rejoice in God; everyone who swears by Him will glory, because the mouth of liars will be stopped.

—PSALM 63:11

The righteous will be glad in the LORD, and seek refuge in Him, and all the upright in heart will glory.

—PSALM 64:10

Sing out the glory of His name; make His praise glorious.

—PSALM 66:2

Sing of the honor and glory and magnificence of His name; make His praise glorious.

—PSALM 66:2, AMP

May God be gracious to us, and bless us, and cause His face to shine on us. Selah

—PSALM 67:1

The earth shook; the heavens also poured down rain at the presence of God; even Sinai shook at the presence of God, the God of Israel.

—PSALM 68:8

The chariots of God are twice ten thousand, even thousands of thousands; the Lord is among them, as in Sinai, in the holy place.

—PSALM 68:17

Blessed be His glorious name forever; and may the whole earth be filled with His glory. Amen, and Amen.

—PSALM 72:19

You will guide me with Your counsel, and afterward receive me to glory.

—PSALM 73:24

You are more glorious and excellent than the mountains of prey.

—PSALM 76:4

The sound of Your thunder was in the whirlwind, and Your lightning lit up the world; the earth trembled and shook.

—PSALM 77:18

And delivered His strength to captivity and His glory into the enemy's hand.

—PSALM 78:61

Help us, O God of our salvation, for the glory of Your name; deliver us, and purge away our sins, for Your name's sake.

—PSALM 79:9

Give ear, O Shepherd of Israel, You who lead Joseph like a flock; You who are enthroned between the cherubim, shine forth.

—PSALM 80:1

You called in trouble, and I delivered you; I answered you in the secret place of thunder; I tested you at the waters of Meribah. Selah.

—Psalm 81:7

For the Lord God is a sun and shield; the Lord will give favor and glory, for no good thing will He withhold from the one who walks uprightly.

—Psalm 84:11

Surely His salvation is near to them who fear Him, that glory may dwell in our land.

—Psalm 85:9

Glorious things are spoken of you, O city of God. Selah.

—Psalm 87:3

For You are the beauty of their strength; by Your favor our horn is exalted.

—Psalm 89:17

You have made his glory cease and cast his throne down to the ground.

—Psalm 89:44

Let Your work be displayed to Your servants and Your glory to their children.

—Psalm 90:16

The Lord reigns; He is robed in majesty; the Lord is robed; He has put on strength as His belt. Indeed, the world is established; it cannot be moved.

—Psalm 93:1

The Lord reigns, He is clothed with majesty and splendor; the Lord has clothed and encircled Himself with strength; the world is firmly established, it cannot be moved.

—Psalm 93:1, amp

Proclaim His glory among the nations, His wonders among all peoples.

—Psalm 96:3

Honor and majesty are before Him; strength and beauty are in His sanctuary. Give unto the Lord, O families of the people, give unto the Lord glory and strength.

—Psalm 96:6–7

Give unto the Lord the glory due His name; bring an offering, and come into His courts.

—Psalm 96:8

Worship the Lord in the splendor of holiness; Tremble [in submissive wonder] before Him, all the earth.

—Psalm 96:9, amp

The mountains melt like wax at the presence of the Lord, at the presence of the Lord of the earth. The heavens declare His righteousness, and all the peoples see His glory.

—Psalm 97:5–6

The Lord reigns; let the peoples tremble! He sits enthroned between the cherubim; let the earth shake.

—Psalm 99:1

So the nations shall fear the name of the Lord, and all the kings of the earth Your glory.

—Psalm 102:15

For the Lord shall build up Zion; He shall appear in His glory.

—Psalm 102:16

Bless the Lord, O my soul! O Lord my God, You are very great! You are clothed with honor and majesty.

—Psalm 104:1

Bless and affectionately praise the Lord, O my soul! O Lord my God, You are very great; You are clothed with splendor and majesty.

—Psalm 104:1, AMP

May the glory of the Lord endure forever; may the Lord rejoice in His works.

—Psalm 104:31

Glory in His holy name; let the heart rejoice for those who seek the Lord.

—Psalm 105:3

Covering Yourself with light as a garment, who stretches out the heavens like a tent curtain.

—Psalm 104:2

That I may see the goodness over Your chosen ones, that I may rejoice in the gladness of Your nation, that I may glory with Your inheritance.

—Psalm 106:5

Thus they changed the glory of God for the image of an ox that eats grass.

—Psalm 106:20

O God, my heart is determined; I will sing and give praise with my whole heart.

—Psalm 108:1

Be exalted, O God, above the heavens, may Your glory be above all the earth.

—Psalm 108:5

Your people will offer themselves willingly [to participate in Your battle] in the day of Your power; In the splendor of holiness, from the womb of the dawn, Your young men are to You as the dew.

—Psalm 110:3, amp

His work is honorable and glorious, and His righteousness endures forever.

—Psalm 111:3

The Lord is high above all nations, and His glory above the heavens.

—Psalm 113:4

Tremble, O earth, at the presence of the Lord, at the presence of the God of Jacob.

—Psalm 114:7

Not unto us, O Lord, not unto us, but unto Your name give glory, for the sake of Your mercy, and for the sake of Your truth.

—Psalm 115:1

Indeed, they shall sing of the ways of the Lord, for great is the glory of the Lord.

—Psalm 138:5

Cast forth lightning, and scatter them; shoot out Your arrows, and destroy them.

—Psalm 144:6

I will speak of the glorious honor of Your majesty and of Your wondrous works.

—Psalm 145:5

They shall speak of the glory of Your kingdom and talk of Your power.

—Psalm 145:11

To make known to people His mighty acts, and the glorious majesty of His kingdom.

—Psalm 145:12

Let them praise the name of the Lord, for His name alone is excellent; His glory is above the earth and heaven.

—Psalm 148:13

Let the godly ones be joyful in glory; let them sing for joy on their beds.

—Psalm 149:5

## Proverbs

The wise will inherit glory, but shame will be the legacy of fools.

—Proverbs 3:35

She will place on your head an ornament of grace; a crown of glory she will deliver to you.

—Proverbs 4:9

The gray-haired head is a crown of glory, if it is found in the way of righteousness.

—Proverbs 16:31

Grandchildren are the crown of old men, and the glory of children are their fathers.

—Proverbs 17:6

The discretion of a man defers his anger, and it is his glory to pass over a transgression.

—Proverbs 19:11

The glory of young men is their strength, and the beauty of old men is the gray head.

—Proverbs 20:29

It is the glory of God to conceal a thing, but the honor of kings is to search out a matter.

—Proverbs 25:2

It is not good to eat much honey; so for men to search their own glory is not glory.

—Proverbs 25:27

When righteous men rejoice, there is great glory; but when the wicked rise, a man hides himself.

—Proverbs 28:12

## Isaiah

Enter into the rock, and hide in the dust from the fear of the Lord and from the glory of His majesty.

—Isaiah 2:10

They shall go into the holes of the rocks, and into the caves of the earth, from the fear of the Lord, and from the glory of His majesty, when He shall arise to shake the earth mightily.

—Isaiah 2:19

To enter the caverns of the rocks, and into the clefts of the cliffs, from the terror of the Lord, and from the glory of His majesty, when He arises to shake the earth mightily.

—Isaiah 2:21

In that day the branch of the Lord shall be beautiful and glorious, and the fruit of the earth shall be excellent and comely for those of Israel who have escaped.

—Isaiah 4:2

Then the Lord will create upon every dwelling place of Mount Zion, and upon her assemblies, a cloud and smoke by day and the shining of a flaming fire by night. For over all the glory shall be a covering.

—Isaiah 4:5

Then the LORD will create over the entire site of Mount Zion and over her assemblies, a cloud by day, smoke, and the brightness of a flaming fire by night; for over all the glory and brilliance will be a canopy [a defense, a covering of His divine love and protection].

—ISAIAH 4:5, AMP

Therefore Sheol has enlarged itself and opened its mouth without measure; so their glory, and their multitude, and their pomp, and he who rejoices shall descend into it.

—ISAIAH 5:14

In the year that King Uzziah died I saw the Lord sitting on a throne, high and lifted up, and His train filled the temple. Above it stood the seraphim. Each one had six wings. With two he covered his face, and with two he covered his feet, and with two he flew. One cried to another and said: "Holy, holy, holy, is the LORD of Hosts; the whole earth is full of His glory." The posts of the door moved at the voice of him who cried, and the house was filled with smoke.

—ISAIAH 6:1–4

Then one of the seraphim flew to me with a live coal which he had taken with the tongs from off the altar in his hand. And he laid it on my mouth, and said, "This has touched your lips, and your iniquity is taken away, and your sin purged."

—ISAIAH 6:6–7

Therefore the Lord, God of Hosts, shall send leanness among his stout ones, and under his glory he shall kindle a burning like the burning of a fire.

—Isaiah 10:16

In that day there shall be a Root of Jesse, who shall stand as a banner to the peoples. For him shall the nations seek. And his rest shall be glorious.

—Isaiah 11:10

I will fasten him as a nail in a firm place, and he shall become a glorious throne to his father's house.

—Isaiah 22:23

They lift up their voices; they sing for the majesty of the Lord; they cry aloud from the west.

—Isaiah 24:14

In that day the Lord of Hosts shall become a crown of glory and a diadem of beauty to the remnant of His people.

—Isaiah 28:5

The Lord shall cause His glorious voice to be heard, and shall show the descending of His arm with the indignation of His anger, and with the flame of a devouring fire, with scattering, and cloudburst, and hailstones.

—Isaiah 30:30

But there the glorious LORD will be to us a place of broad rivers and streams on which no boat with oars shall go and on which no gallant ship shall pass.

—ISAIAH 33:21

It shall blossom abundantly and rejoice even with joy and singing. The glory of Lebanon shall be given to it, the excellency of Carmel and Sharon. They shall see the glory of the LORD and the excellency of our God.

—ISAIAH 35:2

Then the glory of the LORD shall be revealed, and all flesh shall see it together, for the mouth of the LORD has spoken it.

—ISAIAH 40:5

You shall fan them, and the wind shall carry them away, and the whirlwind shall scatter them; and you shall rejoice in the LORD, and shall glory in the Holy One of Israel.

—ISAIAH 41:16

I am the LORD, that is My name; and My glory I will not give to another, nor My praise to graven images.

—ISAIAH 42:8

Let them give glory to the LORD, and declare His praise in the islands.

—ISAIAH 42:12

Even everyone who is called by My name, for I have created him for My glory; I have formed him, and I have made him.

—Isaiah 43:7

In the Lord shall all the seed of Israel be justified and shall glory.

—Isaiah 45:25

I bring My righteousness near; it shall not be far off, and My salvation shall not tarry. And I will grant salvation in Zion, and My glory for Israel.

—Isaiah 46:13

Now says the Lord, who formed me from the womb to be His servant, to bring Jacob back to Him, so that Israel might be gathered to Him (yet I am honored in the eyes of the Lord, and my God is my strength).

—Isaiah 49:5

Then your light shall break forth as the morning, and your healing shall spring forth quickly, and your righteousness shall go before you; the glory of the Lord shall be your reward.

—Isaiah 58:8

So shall they fear the name of the Lord from the west and His glory from the rising of the sun; when the enemy shall come in like a flood, the Spirit of the Lord shall lift up a standard against him.

—Isaiah 59:19

Arise, shine, for your light has come, and the glory of the LORD has risen upon you.

—ISAIAH 60:1

For the darkness shall cover the earth and deep darkness the peoples; but the LORD shall rise upon you, and His glory shall be seen upon you.

—ISAIAH 60:2

The nations shall come to your light and kings to the brightness of your rising.

—ISAIAH 60:3

All the flocks of Kedar shall be gathered together to you, the rams of Nebaioth shall minister to you; they shall come up with acceptance on My altar, and I will glorify My glorious house.

—ISAIAH 60:7

The glory of Lebanon shall come to you, the fir tree, the pine tree, and the box tree together, to beautify the place of My sanctuary; and I will make the place of My feet glorious.

—ISAIAH 60:13

The sun shall no longer be your light by day, nor for brightness shall the moon give light to you; but the LORD shall be an everlasting light to you and your God for your glory.

—ISAIAH 60:19

To preserve those who mourn in Zion, to give to them beauty for ashes, the oil of joy for mourning, the garment of praise for the spirit of heaviness, that they might be called trees of righteousness, the planting of the Lord, that He might be glorified.

—Isaiah 61:3

But you shall be named the priests of the Lord; men shall call you the ministers of our God. You shall eat the riches of the nations, and in their glory you shall boast.

—Isaiah 61:6

For the sake of Zion I will not keep silent, and for the sake of Jerusalem I will not rest until her righteousness goes forth as brightness and her salvation as a lamp that burns.

—Isaiah 62:1

The nations shall see your righteousness, and all kings your glory. And you shall be called by a new name, which the mouth of the Lord shall name.

—Isaiah 62:2

You shall also be a crown of glory in the hand of the Lord and a royal diadem in the hand of your God.

—Isaiah 62:3

Who is this who comes from Edom with dyed garments from Bozrah? This one who is glorious in His apparel, traveling in the greatness of His strength? It is I who speak in righteousness, mighty to save.

—Isaiah 63:1

Who led them with His glorious arm by the right hand of Moses, dividing the water before them, to make Himself an everlasting name.

—Isaiah 63:12

As the cattle which go down into the valley, the Spirit of the Lord caused them to rest, so You led Your people, to make Yourself a glorious name.

—Isaiah 63:14

Look down from heaven and see, from Your holy and glorious habitation. Where are Your zeal and Your strength? The stirrings of Your heart and Your mercies toward me are restrained.

—Isaiah 63:15

Oh, that You would rend the heavens and come down, that the mountains might shake at Your presence, as when the melting fire burns, as the fire causes the waters to boil, to make Your name known to Your adversaries, that the nations may tremble at Your presence! When You did awesome things for which we did not look, You came down; the mountains quaked at Your presence.

—Isaiah 64:1–3

For thus says the Lord: I will extend peace to her like a river and the glory of the nations like a flowing stream. Then you shall nurse, you shall be carried on her sides, and dandled on her knees.

—Isaiah 66:12

For I know their works and their thoughts. The time shall come to gather all nations and tongues. And they shall come and see My glory.

—Isaiah 66:18

I will set a sign among them, and send from them survivors to the nations: to Tarshish, Pul, and Lud—who draw the bow—to Tubal, and Javan, to the coastlands afar off who have not heard My fame nor seen My glory. And they shall declare My glory among the nations.

—Isaiah 66:19

## Jeremiah

Thus says the Lord: Let not the wise man glory in his wisdom, and let not the mighty man glory in his might, let not the rich man glory in his riches; but let him who glories glory in this, that he understands and knows Me, that I am the Lord who exercises lovingkindness, justice, and righteousness in the earth. For in these things I delight, says the Lord.

—Jeremiah 9:23–24

Give glory to the Lord your God, before He causes darkness and before your feet stumble on the dark mountains, and while you look for light, He turns it into the shadow of death and makes it gross darkness.

—Jeremiah 13:16

Say to the king and to the queen mother: "Humble yourselves, sit down, for your beautiful crown shall come down from your head."

—Jeremiah 13:18

Therefore they will come and sing in the height of Zion, and will be joyful over the goodness of the Lord, for wheat and for wine and for oil and for the young of the flock and of the herd; and their souls will be as a watered garden. And they will not sorrow any more at all.

—Jeremiah 31:12

## Ezekiel

As I looked, a whirlwind came out of the north, a great cloud with fire flashing forth continually, and a brightness was all around it, and in its midst something as glowing metal in the midst of the fire.

—Ezekiel 1:4

As for the likeness of the living creatures, their appearance was like burning coals of fire and like the appearance of lamps. It went up and down among the living creatures. And the fire was bright, and out of the fire went forth lightning. The living creatures ran to and fro as the appearance of a flash of lightning.

—Ezekiel 1:13–14

Then I saw as glowing metal, as the appearance of fire all around within it, from the appearance of

His loins and upward; and from the appearance of His loins and downward I saw as it were the appearance of fire, and there was a brightness around Him.

—Ezekiel 1:27

As the appearance of the rainbow that is in the cloud on a day of rain, so was the appearance of the brightness all around. This was the appearance of the likeness of the glory of the Lord. And when I saw it, I fell on my face and heard a voice of one speaking.

—Ezekiel 1:28

Then the Spirit took me up, and I heard behind me a great thundering voice: "Blessed be the glory of the Lord in His place."

—Ezekiel 3:12

Then I arose, and went out into the plain. And the glory of the Lord stood there, as the glory which I saw by the river of Kebar, and I fell on my face.

—Ezekiel 3:23

Then I looked, and there was a likeness as the appearance of a man. From His loins and downward was the appearance of fire. And from His loins and upward was the appearance of brightness, as the appearance of glowing metal.

—Ezekiel 8:2

The glory of the God of Israel was there, according to the vision that I saw in the plain.

—Ezekiel 8:4

Then the glory of the God of Israel ascended from the cherub on which it had been, to the threshold of the temple. And He called to the man clothed with linen who had the writer's case by his side.

—Ezekiel 9:3

Then the glory of the Lord went up from the cherub and stood over the threshold of the temple. And the house was filled with the cloud, and the court was full of the brightness of the glory of the Lord.

—Ezekiel 10:4

Then the glory of the Lord departed from off the threshold of the temple and stood over the cherubim.

—Ezekiel 10:18

The cherubim lifted up their wings and mounted up from the earth in my sight. When they went out, the wheels were beside them. They stood at the door of the east gate of the house of the Lord; and the glory of the God of Israel was above them.

—Ezekiel 10:19

Then the cherubim lifted up their wings with the wheels beside them. And the glory of the God of Israel was over them.

—Ezekiel 11:22

The glory of the Lord went up from the midst of the city and stood on the mountain which is on the east side of the city.

—Ezekiel 11:23

I will set My glory among the nations, and all the nations shall see My judgment that I have executed, and My hand that I have laid upon them.

—Ezekiel 39:21

And the glory of the God of Israel came from the way of the east. And His voice was like a noise of many waters. And the earth shone with His glory.

—Ezekiel 43:2

The glory of the Lord came into the temple by the way of the gate facing east.

—Ezekiel 43:4

So the Spirit took me up and brought me into the inner court. And the glory of the Lord filled the temple.

—Ezekiel 43:5

Then he brought me by the way of the north gate before the temple. And I looked, and the glory of the Lord filled the house of the Lord, and I fell upon my face.

—Ezekiel 44:4

## Daniel

At the same time my reason returned to me. And for the glory of my kingdom, my honor and splendor returned to me. And my counselors and my lords sought me out. Then I was established in my kingdom, and excellent majesty was added to me.

—Daniel 4:36

And for the majesty that He gave him, all peoples, nations, and languages trembled and feared before him. Whom he would, he slaughtered, and whom he would, he kept alive; whom he would, he set up, and whom he would, he put down.

—Daniel 5:19

There was given to Him dominion, and glory, and a kingdom, that all peoples, nations, and languages should serve Him. His dominion is an everlasting dominion, which shall not pass away, and His kingdom that which shall not be destroyed.

—Daniel 7:14

Those who are wise shall shine as the brightness of the expanse of heaven, and those who turn the many to righteousness as the stars forever and ever.

—Daniel 12:3

## Jonah

But Jonah got up to flee to Tarshish from the presence of the Lord. He went down to Joppa and found there a ship going to Tarshish. He paid its fare and went down into it to go with them to Tarshish from the presence of the LORD.

—JONAH 1:3

Then the men were very afraid and said to him, "What is this you have done?" For the men knew that he was fleeing from the presence of the LORD because he had told them.

—JONAH 1:10

## Nahum

The mountains quake before Him, and the hills melt; the land rises up before Him, the earth and everything that dwells on it.

—NAHUM 1:5

## Habakkuk

For the earth will be filled with the knowledge of the glory of the LORD, as the waters cover the seas.

—HABAKKUK 2:14

God [approaching from Sinai] comes from Teman (Edom), and the Holy One from Mount Paran. Selah (pause, and calmly think of that). His splendor and majesty covers the heavens and the earth is full of His praise.

—HABAKKUK 3:3, AMP

His brightness was like the light; rays flashed from His hand, and there His power was hidden.

—HABAKKUK 3:4

## Zephaniah

Be silent before the Lord GOD! For the day of the LORD is at hand; the LORD has prepared the sacrifice; He has consecrated His guests.

—ZEPHANIAH 1:7

## Haggai

And I will shake all the nations, and they will come with the wealth of all nations, and I will fill this house with glory, says the LORD of Hosts.

—HAGGAI 2:7

The glory of this latter house will be greater than the former, says the LORD of Hosts. And in this place I will give peace, says the LORD of Hosts.

—HAGGAI 2:9

## Zechariah

And I will be like a wall of fire all around her, says the LORD, and I will be as glory in her midst.

—ZECHARIAH 2:5

For thus says the Lord of Hosts: He has sent Me
after glory to the nations which plunder you, for he
who touches you touches the apple of His eye.

—Zechariah 2:8

It is he who shall build the temple of the Lord; he
shall bear the glory, and shall sit and rule on his
throne. He shall be a priest on his throne, and the
counsel of peace shall be between them both.

—Zechariah 6:13

Then the Lord will appear over them, and His
arrow will go out like lightning. The Lord God
will sound His trumpet, and will march forth like
storm winds of southern Teman.

—Zechariah 9:14

Ask for rain from the Lord during the season of
the latter spring rains. And the Lord will make
the storm winds; and He will give them showers of
rain; all will have vegetation in the field.

—Zechariah 10:1

The Lord will deliver the tents of Judah as before,
so that the glory of the house of David and the
glory of those dwelling in Jerusalem will not eclipse
Judah.

—Zechariah 12:7

## Malachi

If you will not listen, and if you will not take it to heart to give honor to My name, says the LORD of Hosts, I will send a curse on you and I will curse your blessings. Yes, I have cursed them already, because you do not take it to heart.

—MALACHI 2:2

# 9

# GOD IN THE NEW TESTAMENT

The glory of God is the manifest presence of God. We get the benefits of the nature of God through His presence. God's glory is radiant, magnificent, brilliant, majestic, splendorous, and beautiful. When we are in the presence of God, we feel His love and faithfulness. We feel empowered, bold, and courageous. Like the apostles in the New Testament church, we are able to do supernatural exploits all because we've sat under the covering of His glory.

The Greek word for glory is *doxa*, meaning "honor, renown; glory, an especially divine quality, the unspoken manifestation of God, splendor."[1] It also means "splendour, brightness," and "majesty," expressed in these three ways:

1. "A thing belonging to God"—"the kingly
   majesty which belongs to him as supreme

ruler, majesty in the sense of the absolute perfection of the deity"

2. "A thing belonging to Christ"—"the kingly majesty of the Messiah"; "the absolutely perfect inward or personal excellency of Christ; the majesty"

3. "A most glorious condition, most exalted state"—"of that condition with God the Father in heaven to which Christ was raised after he had achieved his work on earth"; and "the glorious condition of blessedness into which is appointed and promised that true Christians shall enter after their Saviour's return from heaven."[2]

The key verse for this chapter is 2 Corinthians 3:18, "But we all, seeing the glory of the Lord with unveiled faces, as in a mirror, are being transformed into the same image from glory to glory by the Spirit of the Lord."

## Matthew

Again, the devil took Him up on a very high mountain and showed Him all the kingdoms of the world and their grandeur, and said to Him, "All these things I will give You if You will fall down and worship me."

—MATTHEW 4:8–9

Therefore, when you do your charitable deeds, do not sound a trumpet before you as the hypocrites do in the synagogues and in the streets, that they may be honored by men. Truly I say to you, they have their reward.

—MATTHEW 6:2

And lead us not into temptation, but deliver us from evil. For Yours is the kingdom and the power and the glory forever. Amen.

—MATTHEW 6:13

Yet I say to you that even Solomon in all his glory was not dressed like one of these.

—MATTHEW 6:29

For the Son of Man shall come with His angels in the glory of His Father, and then He will repay every man according to his works.

—MATTHEW 16:27

While he was still speaking, suddenly a bright cloud overshadowed them, and a voice from the cloud said, "This is My beloved Son, with whom I am well pleased. Listen to Him."

—MATTHEW 17:5

Jesus said to them, "Truly I say to you, in the regeneration, when the Son of Man sits on His glorious throne, you who have followed Me will also sit on twelve thrones, judging the twelve tribes of Israel."

—MATTHEW 19:28

Then the sign of the Son of Man will appear in heaven, and then all the tribes of the earth will mourn, and they will see the Son of Man coming on the clouds of heaven with power and great glory.

—MATTHEW 24:30

When the Son of Man comes in His glory, and all the holy angels with Him, then He will sit on the throne of His glory.

—MATTHEW 25:31

And then there was a great earthquake. For the angel of the Lord descended from heaven and came and rolled back the stone from the door and sat on it. His countenance was like lightning, and his garments white as snow. The soldiers shook for fear of him and became like dead men.

—MATTHEW 28:2–4

## Mark

Whoever therefore is ashamed of Me and of My words in this adulterous and sinful generation, of him will the Son of Man also be ashamed when He comes in the glory of His Father with the holy angels.

—MARK 8:38

And His clothes became radiant and dazzling, intensely white, as no launderer on earth can whiten them.

—MARK 9:3, AMP

They said to Him, "Grant us to sit, one at Your right hand and the other at Your left hand, in Your glory."

—Mark 10:37

Then they will see the Son of Man coming in clouds with great power and glory.

—Mark 13:26

## Luke

The angel answered him, "I am Gabriel, who stands in the presence of God. And I was sent to speak to you and to bring you this good news."

—Luke 1:19

And then an angel of the Lord appeared to them, and the glory of the Lord shone around them, and they were very afraid.

—Luke 2:9

Glory to God in the highest, and on earth peace, and good will toward men.

—Luke 2:14

A light for revelation to the Gentiles, and the glory of Your people Israel.

—Luke 2:32

And the devil said to Him, "I will give You all this power and their glory, for it has been delivered to me. And I give it to whomever I will."

—Luke 4:6

For whoever is ashamed of Me and My words, of him will the Son of Man be ashamed when He comes in His own glory and in the glory of His Father and of the holy angels.

—LUKE 9:26

Who appeared in glory and spoke of His departure which He was to accomplish in Jerusalem.

—LUKE 9:31

Peter and those who were with him were heavy with sleep. But waking thoroughly, they saw His glory and the two men who stood with Him.

—LUKE 9:32

If your whole body, then, is full of light, no part being dark, the whole body will be full of light, as when the shining candle gives you light.

—LUKE 11:36

Consider how the lilies grow. They neither spin nor weave. Yet I say to you that Solomon in all his glory was not arrayed like one of these.

—LUKE 12:27

When He said this, all His adversaries were ashamed. And all the people rejoiced for all the glorious things that were done by Him.

—LUKE 13:17

Were there not any found to return and give glory to God except this foreigner?

—LUKE 17:18

Saying: "Blessed is the King who comes in the name of the Lord!" Peace in heaven and glory in the highest!

—Luke 19:38

Then they will see the Son of Man coming in a cloud with power and great glory.

—Luke 21:27

Was it not necessary for the Christ to suffer these things and to enter His glory?

—Luke 24:26

## John

The Word became flesh and dwelt among us, and we saw His glory, the glory as the only Son of the Father, full of grace and truth.

—John 1:14

This, the first of His signs, Jesus did in Cana of Galilee, and He revealed His glory, and His disciples believed in Him.

—John 2:11

He who speaks on his own authority seeks his own glory. But He who seeks the glory of Him who sent Him is true, and no unrighteousness is in Him.

—John 7:18

I do not seek glory for Myself. There is One who seeks it and judges.

—John 8:50

When Jesus heard this, He said, "This sickness is not unto death, but for the glory of God, that the Son of God may be glorified by it."

—JOHN 11:4

Jesus said to her, "Did I not tell you that if you believed, you would see the glory of God?"

—JOHN 11:40

Isaiah said this when he saw His glory and spoke of Him.

—JOHN 12:41

And now, O Father, glorify Me in Your own presence with the glory which I had with You before the world existed.

—JOHN 17:5

I have given them the glory which You gave Me, that they may be one even as We are one.

—JOHN 17:22

Father, I desire that they also, whom You have given Me, be with Me where I am, that they may see My glory which You have given Me. For You loved Me before the creation of the world.

—JOHN 17:24

## Acts

He said, "Brothers and fathers, listen! The God of glory appeared to our father Abraham, when he was in Mesopotamia, before he lived in Harran."

—Acts 7:2

But being full of the Holy Spirit, he gazed into heaven and saw the glory of God, and Jesus standing at the right hand of God.

—Acts 7:55

Immediately an angel of the Lord struck him, because he did not give God the glory. And he was eaten by worms and died.

—Acts 12:23

Since I was blinded by the glory of that light, those who were with me led me by the hand into Damascus.

—Acts 22:11

At midday, O King, I saw along the way a light from heaven, brighter than the sun, shining around me and those who journeyed with me.

—Acts 26:13

## Romans

They changed the glory of the incorruptible God into an image made like corruptible man, birds, four-footed beasts, and creeping things.

—Romans 1:23

To those who by patiently doing good seek for glory and honor and immortality will be eternal life.

—ROMANS 2:7

But glory, honor, and peace will be to every man who does good work—to the Jew first, and then to the Gentile.

—ROMANS 2:10

For all have sinned and come short of the glory of God.

—ROMANS 3:23

If Abraham was justified by works, he has something to boast about, but not before God.

—ROMANS 4:2

He did not waver at the promise of God through unbelief, but was strong in faith, giving glory to God.

—ROMANS 4:20

Through whom we also have access by faith into this grace in which we stand, and so we rejoice in hope of the glory of God.

—ROMANS 5:2

For I consider that the sufferings of this present time are not worthy to be compared with the glory which shall be revealed to us.

—ROMANS 8:18

That the creation itself also will be set free from its slavery to corruption into the glorious freedom of the children of God.

—ROMANS 8:21

Who are Israelites, to whom belong the adoption, the glory, the covenants, the giving of the law, the service of God, and the promises.

—ROMANS 9:4

In order to make known the riches of His glory on the vessels of mercy, which He previously prepared for glory.

—ROMANS 9:23

For from Him and through Him and to Him are all things. To Him be glory forever! Amen.

—ROMANS 11:36

Therefore welcome one another, just as Christ also welcomed us, for the glory of God.

—ROMANS 15:7

To the only wise God, through Jesus Christ, to whom be glory forever. Amen.

—ROMANS 16:27

# 1 Corinthians

So that no flesh should boast in His presence.

—1 CORINTHIANS 1:29

Therefore, as it is written, "Let him who boasts, boast in the Lord."

—1 Corinthians 1:31

But we speak the wisdom of God in a mystery, the hidden wisdom, which God ordained before the ages for our glory.

—1 Corinthians 2:7

None of the rulers of this age knew it. For had they known it, they would not have crucified the Lord of glory.

—1 Corinthians 2:8

Therefore let no one boast in men. For all things are yours.

—1 Corinthians 3:21

For who makes you differ from another? And what do you have that you did not receive? Now if you received it, why do you boast as if you had not received it?

—1 Corinthians 4:7

Your boasting is not good. Do you not know that a little yeast leavens the whole batch?

—1 Corinthians 5:6

Though I preach the gospel, I have nothing to boast of, for the requirement is laid upon me. Yes, woe unto me if I do not preach the gospel!

—1 Corinthians 9:16

Therefore, whether you eat, or drink, or whatever you do, do it all to the glory of God.

—1 Corinthians 10:31

There are also celestial bodies and terrestrial bodies. The glory of the celestial is one, and the glory of the terrestrial is another.

—1 Corinthians 15:40

There is one glory of the sun, and another glory of the moon, and another glory of the stars. One star differs from another star in glory.

—1 Corinthians 15:41

It is sown in dishonor, it is raised in glory. It is sown in weakness, it is raised in power.

—1 Corinthians 15:43

## 2 Corinthians

For all the promises of God in Him are "Yes," and in Him "Amen," to the glory of God through us.

—2 Corinthians 1:20

If the ministry that brought death, written and engraved on stones, was glorious, so that the children of Israel could not look intently at the face of Moses because of the glory of his countenance, the glory which was to fade away, how will the ministry of the Spirit not be more glorious?

—2 Corinthians 3:7–8

For if the ministry of condemnation is glorious, the ministry of righteousness much more exceeds it in glory.

—2 CORINTHIANS 3:9

Even that which was made glorious had no glory in comparison to the glory that excels.

—2 CORINTHIANS 3:10

But we all, seeing the glory of the Lord with unveiled faces, as in a mirror, are being transformed into the same image from glory to glory by the Spirit of the Lord.

—2 CORINTHIANS 3:18

For God, who commanded the light to shine out of darkness, has shone in our hearts to give the light of the knowledge of the glory of God in the face of Jesus Christ.

—2 CORINTHIANS 4:6

But we have this precious treasure [the good news about salvation] in [unworthy] earthen vessels [of human frailty], so that the grandeur and surpassing greatness of the power will be [shown to be] from God [His sufficiency] and not from ourselves.

—2 CORINTHIANS 4:7, AMP

All these things are for your sakes, so that the abundant grace through the thanksgiving of many might overflow to the glory of God.

—2 CORINTHIANS 4:15

Our light affliction, which lasts but for a moment, works for us a far more exceeding and eternal weight of glory.

—2 Corinthians 4:17

Let him who boasts, boast in the Lord.

—2 Corinthians 10:17

If I must boast, I will boast of the things which concern my weakness.

—2 Corinthians 11:30

Doubtless it is not profitable for me to boast. So I will move on to visions and revelations of the Lord.

—2 Corinthians 12:1

Of such a person, I will boast. Yet of myself I will not boast, except in my weaknesses.

—2 Corinthians 12:5

For if I desire to boast, I will not be a fool, for I will be speaking the truth. But now I resist, lest anyone should think of me above that which he sees me to be or hears from me.

—2 Corinthians 12:6

But He said to me, "My grace is sufficient for you, for My strength is made perfect in weakness." Therefore most gladly I will boast in my weaknesses, that the power of Christ may rest upon me.

—2 Corinthians 12:9

I have become a fool in boasting. You have compelled me, for I ought to have been commended by you, for I am in no way inferior to the leading apostles, though I am nothing.

—2 Corinthians 12:11

## Galatians

To whom be glory forever and ever. Amen.

—Galatians 1:5

Let us not be conceited, provoking one another and envying one another.

—Galatians 5:26

For they themselves who are circumcised do not keep the law. But they desire to have you circumcised, so that they may boast in your flesh.

—Galatians 6:13

God forbid that I should boast, except in the cross of our Lord Jesus Christ, by whom the world is crucified to me, and I to the world.

—Galatians 6:14

## Ephesians

To the praise of the glory of His grace which He graciously bestowed on us in the Beloved.

—Ephesians 1:6

Who is the guarantee of our inheritance until the redemption of the purchased possession, to the praise of His glory.

—Ephesians 1:14

So that the God of our Lord Jesus Christ, the Father of glory, may give you the Spirit of wisdom and revelation in the knowledge of Him.

—Ephesians 1:17

That the eyes of your understanding may be enlightened, that you may know what is the hope of His calling and what are the riches of the glory of His inheritance among the saints.

—Ephesians 1:18

That He would give you, according to the riches of His glory, power to be strengthened by His Spirit in the inner man.

—Ephesians 3:16

To Him be the glory in the church and in Christ Jesus throughout all generations, forever and ever. Amen.

—Ephesians 3:21

And that He might present to Himself a glorious church, not having spot, or wrinkle, or any such thing, but that it should be holy and without blemish.

—Ephesians 5:27

## Philippians

Being filled with the fruit of righteousness, which comes through Jesus Christ, for the glory and praise of God.

—PHILIPPIANS 1:11

And every tongue should confess that Jesus Christ is Lord, to the glory of God the Father.

—PHILIPPIANS 2:11

Who will transform our body of humiliation, so that it may be conformed to His glorious body, according to the working of His power even to subdue all things to Himself.

—PHILIPPIANS 3:21

But my God shall supply your every need according to His riches in glory by Christ Jesus.

—PHILIPPIANS 4:19

Now to God and our Father be glory forever and ever. Amen.

—PHILIPPIANS 4:20

## Colossians

Strengthened with all might according to His glorious power, enduring everything with perseverance and patience joyfully.

—COLOSSIANS 1:11

To them God would make known what is the glorious riches of this mystery among the nations. It is Christ in you, the hope of glory.

—Colossians 1:27

When Christ who is our life shall appear, then you also shall appear with Him in glory.

—Colossians 3:4

## 1 Thessalonians

Nor did we seek glory from men, either from you, or from others, even though we might have made demands as the apostles of Christ.

—1 Thessalonians 2:6

That you would walk in a manner worthy of God, who has called you to His kingdom and glory.

—1 Thessalonians 2:12

You are our glory and joy.

—1 Thessalonians 2:20

## 2 Thessalonians

So we boast about you in the churches of God for your patience and faith in all your persecutions and tribulations that you are enduring.

—2 Thessalonians 1:4

They shall be punished with eternal destruction, isolated from the presence of the Lord and from the glory of His power.

—2 Thessalonians 1:9

Then the lawless one will be revealed, whom the Lord will consume with the breath of His mouth, and destroy with the brightness of His presence.

—2 Thessalonians 2:8

To this He called you by our gospel, to obtain the glory of our Lord Jesus Christ.

—2 Thessalonians 2:14

## 1 Timothy

According to the glorious gospel of the blessed God, which was committed to my trust.

—1 Timothy 1:11

Now to the eternal, immortal, invisible King, the only wise God, be honor and glory forever. Amen.

—1 Timothy 1:17

Without question, great is the mystery of godliness: God was revealed in the flesh, justified in the Spirit, seen by angels, preached to the Gentiles, believed on in the world, taken up into glory.

—1 Timothy 3:16

He alone has immortality, living in unapproachable light, whom no one has seen, nor can see. To Him be honor and everlasting power. Amen.

—1 Timothy 6:16

## 2 Timothy

Therefore I endure all things for the sake of the elect, that they also may obtain the salvation which is in Christ Jesus with eternal glory.

—2 Timothy 2:10

The Lord will deliver me from every evil work and will preserve me for His heavenly kingdom, to whom be glory forever and ever. Amen.

—2 Timothy 4:18

## Hebrews

He is the brightness of His glory, the express image of Himself, and upholds all things by the word of His power. When He had by Himself purged our sins, He sat down at the right hand of the Majesty on high.

—Hebrews 1:3

You made him a little lower than the angels; You crowned him with glory and honor, and set him over the works of Your hands.

—Hebrews 2:7

But we see Jesus, who was made a little lower than the angels to suffer death, crowned with glory and honor, so that He, by the grace of God, should experience death for everyone.

—HEBREWS 2:9

For it was fitting for Him, for whom and by whom all things exist, in bringing many sons to glory, to make the Author of their salvation perfect through suffering.

—HEBREWS 2:10

For the One was counted worthy of more glory than Moses, in that He who builds the house has more honor than the house itself.

—HEBREWS 3:3

Now this is the main point of the things that we are saying: We have such a High Priest, who is seated at the right hand of the throne of the Majesty in the heavens.

—HEBREWS 8:1

Above the ark were the cherubim of glory overshadowing the mercy seat. Concerning these things we cannot now speak in detail.

—HEBREWS 9:5

For Christ did not enter holy places made with hands, which are patterned after the true one, but into heaven itself, now to appear in the presence of God for us.

—HEBREWS 9:24

May the God of peace…make you perfect in every good work to do His will, working in you that which is pleasing in His sight, through Jesus Christ, to whom be glory forever and ever. Amen.

—Hebrews 13:20–21

## James

My brothers, have faith in our Lord Jesus Christ, the Lord of glory, without partiality.

—James 2:1

## 1 Peter

In order that the genuineness of your faith, which is more precious than gold that perishes, though it is tried by fire, may be found to result in praise, glory, and honor at the revelation of Jesus Christ.

—1 Peter 1:7

Whom, having not seen, you love; and in whom, though you do not see Him now, you believe and you rejoice with joy unspeakable and full of glory.

—1 Peter 1:8

Seeking the events and time the Spirit of Christ, who was within them, signified when He foretold the sufferings of Christ and the glories to follow.

—1 Peter 1:11

Through Him you believe in God who raised Him up from the dead and gave Him glory, so that your faith and hope might be in God.

—1 Peter 1:21

All flesh is as grass, and all the glory of man as the flower of grass. The grass withers, and its flower falls away.

—1 Peter 1:24

But rejoice insofar as you share in Christ's sufferings, so that you may rejoice and be glad also in the revelation of His glory.

—1 Peter 4:13

If you are reproached because of the name of Christ, you are blessed, because the Spirit of glory and of God rests upon you. On their part He is blasphemed, but on your part He is glorified.

—1 Peter 4:14

I exhort the elders who are among you, as one who is also an elder and a witness of the sufferings of Christ as well as a partaker of the glory that shall be revealed.

—1 Peter 5:1

And when the chief Shepherd appears, you will receive a crown of glory that will not fade away.

—1 Peter 5:4

But after you have suffered a little while, the God of all grace, who has called us to His eternal glory through Christ Jesus, will restore, support, strengthen, and establish you.

—1 Peter 5:10

To Him be glory and dominion forever and ever. Amen.

—1 Peter 5:11

## 2 Peter

His divine power has given to us all things that pertain to life and godliness through the knowledge of Him who has called us by His own glory and excellence.

—2 Peter 1:3

For we have not followed cleverly devised myths when we made known to you the power and coming of our Lord Jesus Christ, but we were eyewitnesses of His majesty. For He received honor and glory from God the Father when a voice came to Him from the majestic glory, saying, "This is My beloved Son, in whom I am well pleased."

—2 Peter 1:16–17

But grow in the grace and knowledge of our Lord and Savior Jesus Christ. To Him be glory, both now and forever. Amen.

—2 Peter 3:18

## Jude

Now to Him who is able to keep you from falling and to present you blameless before the presence of His glory with rejoicing, to the only wise God our Savior, be glory and majesty, dominion and power, both now and forever. Amen.

—Jude 24–25

## Revelation

And has made us kings and priests to His God and Father, to Him be glory and dominion forever and ever. Amen.

—Revelation 1:6

Lightnings and thunderings and voices proceeded from the throne. Seven lamps of fire were burning before the throne, which are the seven Spirits of God.

—Revelation 4:5

The living creatures give glory and honor and thanks to Him who sits on the throne, who lives forever and ever.

—Revelation 4:9

You are worthy, O Lord, to receive glory and honor and power; for You have created all things, and by Your will they exist and were created.

—Revelation 4:11

Saying with a loud voice: "Worthy is the Lamb who was slain, to receive power and riches and wisdom and strength and honor and glory and blessing!"

—Revelation 5:12

Then I heard every creature which is in heaven and on the earth and under the earth and in the sea, and all that are in them, saying: "To Him who sits on the throne and to the Lamb be blessing and honor and glory and power, forever and ever!"

—Revelation 5:13

Saying: "Amen! Blessing and glory and wisdom and thanksgiving and honor and power and might be to our God forever and ever! Amen."

—Revelation 7:12

At that same hour there was a great earthquake, and a tenth of the city fell. Seven thousand men were killed in the earthquake, and the remnant were frightened and gave glory to the God of heaven.

—Revelation 11:13

Then the temple of God was opened in heaven, and the ark of His covenant was seen in His temple. And there came lightning, noises, thundering, an earthquake, and great hail.

—Revelation 11:19

He said with a loud voice, "Fear God and give Him glory, for the hour of His judgment has come.

Worship Him who made heaven and earth, the sea
and the springs of water."

—REVELATION 14:7

And the temple was filled with smoke from the
glory of God and from His power. No one was able
to enter the temple until the seven plagues of the
seven angels were completed.

—REVELATION 15:8

Men were scorched with great heat, and they blasphemed the name of God who has power over these
plagues, and they did not repent and give Him
glory.

—REVELATION 16:9

After this I saw another angel coming down from
heaven, having great authority, and the earth was
illuminated with his glory.

—REVELATION 18:1

After these things I heard a great sound of many
people in heaven, shouting: "Alleluia! Salvation
and glory and honor and power belong to the Lord
our God!"

—REVELATION 19:1

Having the glory of God, her light like a most precious jewel, like a jasper, clear as crystal.

—REVELATION 21:11

Having God's glory [filled with His radiant light].
The brilliance of it resembled a rare and very

precious jewel, like jasper, shining and clear as
crystal.

—Revelation 21:11, amp

The city has no need of sun or moon to shine in
it, for the glory of God is its light, and its lamp is
the Lamb.

—Revelation 21:23

And the nations of those who are saved shall walk
in its light, and the kings of the earth shall bring
their glory and honor into it.

—Revelation 21:24

They shall bring into it the glory and the honor of
the nations.

—Revelation 21:26

I, Jesus, have sent My angel to you with this testimony for the churches. I am the Root and the
Offspring of David, the Bright and Morning Star.

—Revelation 22:16

# NOTES

## Chapter 2
## Worship in the Old Testament

1. W. Marcus Bevans, *The Truth About Worship* (n.p.: BookBaby, 2012).

## Chapter 3
## Worship in the New Testament

1. BlueLetterBible.org, s.v. "*proskyneō*," accessed December 13, 2017, https://www.blueletterbible.org/lang/lexicon/lexicon.cfm?Strongs=G4352&t=KJV.

2. BlueLetterBible.org, s.v. "*sebō*," accessed December 13, 2017, https://www.blueletterbible.org/lang/lexicon/lexicon.cfm?Strongs=G4576&t=KJV.

3. BlueLetterBible.org, s.v. "*eusebeō*," accessed December 13, 2017, https://www.blueletterbible.org/lang/lexicon/lexicon.cfm?Strongs=G2151&t=KJV.

4. BlueLetterBible.org, s.v. "*ethelothrēskia*," accessed December 13, 2017, https://www.blueletterbible.org/lang/lexicon/lexicon.cfm?Strongs=G1479&t=KJV.

5. BlueLetterBible.org, s.v. "*latreuō*," accessed December 13, 2017, https://www.blueletterbible.org/lang/lexicon/lexicon.cfm?Strongs=G3000&t=KJV.

6. BlueLetterBible.org, s.v. *"piptō,"* accessed December 13, 2017, https://www.blueletterbible.org/lang/lexicon/lexicon.cfm?Strongs=G4098&t=KJV.

## Chapter 4
### Be Holy as I Am Holy

1. Merriam-Webter.com, s.v. "holiness," accessed December 13, 2017, https://www.merriam-webster.com/dictionary/holiness.

2. Merriam-Webter.com, s.v. "holy," accessed December 13, 2017, https://www.merriam-webster.com/dictionary/holy.

3. Dictionary.com, s.v. "holy," accessed December 13, 2017, http://www.dictionary.com/browse/holy.

## Chapter 5
### Holiness in the Old Testament

1. BlueLetterBible.org, s.v. *"qodesh,"* accessed December 13, 2017, https://www.blueletterbible.org/lang/lexicon/lexicon.cfm?Strongs=H6944&t=KJV.

2. BlueLetterBible.org, s.v. *"qodesh."*

3. BlueLetterBible.org, s.v. *"qadash,"* accessed December 13, 2017, https://www.blueletterbible.org/lang/lexicon/lexicon.cfm?strongs=H6942&t=KJV.

## Chapter 6
### Holiness in the New Testament

1. BlueLetterBible.org, s.v. *"hagios,"* accessed December 13, 2017, https://www.blueletterbible.org/lang/lexicon/lexicon.cfm?Strongs=G40&t=KJV.

2. BibleHub.com, s.v. "40. *hagios*," accessed December 13, 2017, http://biblehub.com/greek/40.htm.

## CHAPTER 7
### THERE IS NONE LIKE YOU

1. "The Names of God in the Old Testament," BlueLetterBible.org, accessed December 13, 2017, https://www.blueletterbible.org/study/misc/name_god.cfm.

2. *Oxford Living Dictionaries*, s.v. "wonderful," accessed January 1, 2018, https://en.oxforddictionaries.com/definition/wonderful.

3. CollinsDictionary.com, s.v. "radiant," accessed December 13, 2017, https://www.collinsdictionary.com/us/dictionary/english/radiant.

## CHAPTER 8
### GOD IN THE OLD TESTAMENT

1. BlueLetterBible.org, s.v. "*kabowd*," accessed December 13, 2017, https://www.blueletterbible.org/lang/lexicon/lexicon.cfm?strongs=h3519.

2. BlueLetterBible.org, s.v. "*kabowd*."

3. *Nave's Topical Bible*, s.v. "*shekinah*," accessed December 13, 2017, https://www.blueletterbible.org/search/Dictionary/viewTopic.cfm?topic=NT0004430.

4. BlueLetterBible.org, s.v. "*no'am*," accessed December 13, 2017, https://www.blueletterbible.org/lang/lexicon/lexicon.cfm?t=kjv&strongs=h5278.

## Chapter 9
### God in the New Testament

1. BibleHub.com, s.v. "*doxa*," accessed December 13, 2017, http://biblehub.com/greek/1391.htm.

2. BlueLetterBible.org, s.v. "*doxa*," accessed December 13, 2017, https://www.blueletterbible.org/lang/lexicon/lexicon.cfm?Strongs=G1391&t=KJV.